WHOLE AGAIN

Lee Whipple

Caroline House Publishers, Inc.
Ottawa, Illinois & Ossining, New York

Caroline House Publishers, Inc.
Post Office Box 738, Ottawa, IL 61350

Library of Congress Catalogue Card Number: 80-81034

ISBN: 0-89803-023-4

Manufactured in the United States of America

WHOLE AGAIN

*Dedicated to all those
who refuse to be told
there is not a way.*

CONTENTS

Part Three: 1974-
Chapter

Part One

1970–

1

Joliet, Illinois, June 2, 1970, A.M. It is quiet in the Black Road apartment complex. Black Road is the interracial brainchild of millionaire land developer and representative to the Illinois legislature. William G. Barr. The Black Road development is not popular.

Bill Barr himself lives in a Black Road apartment. It is not the standard unit. Designed into the complex, it appears the same. But it is larger by several times and furnished luxuriously. Still, Barr's political point is made.

He has watched crosses burn on his lawn on three separate occasions.

The night before, Bill worked late at his legislative office and returned to the Black Road apartment. In the middle of his fourth divorce, he lives alone.

He sleeps later than intended. He is in a hurry as he shaves and dresses. Bill is a large man, young for his fifty years, good looking, confident in his movements. His clothes are expensive; the press has a habit of referring to him as a "flamboyant, millionaire legislator." He has no quarrel with this.

Bill walks the seventy-five feet from his door to the waiting Cadillac. It is a light green DeVille parked in a long open carport. He opens the door and slides behind the wheel, leaving his left foot flat on the driveway. This is the way he has always started a car; he does not know why himself. His friends and subsequently the press will comment on it many times in the next few days.

Beneath the hood, five dull-brown sticks of dynamite are clustered about the steering column; this places them approximately forty inches in front of and below the driver. The dynamite is wired directly into the ignition system. It is a professional job.

Bill inserts his key in the ignition, rotating it clockwise with his thumb and first finger. It is fully intended that this be the last motion of his life. . .

The explosion rattled windows in a fourteen-block area. Cars on nearby Larkin Avenue stopped, the drivers confused and unsettled by the noise. Nick Murphy, a Barr associate, watched the dishes on the breakfast table in his second-story Black Road apartment tremble; he looked out of his window into a cloud of black smoke.

Bill Barr had stepped into an erupting volcano. A stick of dynamite explodes with the force of a million pounds per square inch. The roof of the carport above the car was blown completely off. The hood of the car landed 150 feet away. Scattered pieces of metal and glass rained down 300 feet from the site of the original explosion.

Bill felt himself lifted up, suspended above the ground. He heard the explosion as if it originated within his own body. Then there was pain, his own private universe of pain.

2

Nick Murphy ran from his apartment. It was less than three minutes since the explosion. Bill Barr was lying on his back several body lengths from the mangled steel that had been his car. A young black woman was holding his head. She was strangely calm, perhaps in shock.

Smoke was rising through the jagged remains of the carport roof. A nearby fence had been ripped open, exposing the unpainted insides of broken and twisted boards. Scraps of metal and glass covered the ground.

Nick ran the hundred feet from the apartment building door to Bill's body. He was close now.

Bill's face was a mask of red. His right leg was torn open, the bones of his knee and lower leg seemed almost white against the dark pavement; the upper leg was bathed in blood. Blood was spurting from beneath the remains of his pantleg, beginning to pool beneath him.

Bill recognized Nick through a haze of shock and disbelief. His mind wouldn't guess what had happened. Something had blown. Something big. He had been in the way. That was all.

But his leg, he could feel that.

"Ambulance," Bill shouted. "Get an ambulance. . . Call the office, tell them what happened. Tell them I won't be in. . . Your shirt, make a tourniquet. Put a tourniquet on my leg. . . Morphine, get morphine. Quick."

Nick was already tearing off his shirt, reaching around the remains of Bill's leg. He tied the shirt near the top of the thigh. The blood soaked quickly through the material. Blood spurted against Nick's bare midriff and soaked into his pants. He didn't notice.

He pulled the tourniquet tight, tighter. The bleeding began to slow. Sirens were in the distance.

Call the office, Nick thought, *call the office—how can he think of that, now?*

Sirens, loud: firetrucks, ambulance, police. They all seemed to come at once. Nick was pushed gently aside. Bill was unconscious now. Two men in white lifted him onto a stretcher.

It had started to rain. A crowd had gathered. Nick noticed both for the first time.

They were loading Bill into the ambulance. Police began to move the crowd back; they were putting up ropes around the whole area.

The ambulance doors closed, the flashers began. Then the siren. The ambulance pulled around slowly, making its way into the street; it gained speed quickly. The intensity of the siren increased. And the ambulance was gone. Nick could still hear it for a while. Then, that too was gone.

June 3. The headlines in dozens of papers read—

WILLIAM G. BARR BOMBED IN AUTO
CRITICALLY INJURED

Governor Richard Ogilvie called in the IBI (Illinois Bureau of Investigation) and the state police. Political notables from across the country were flooding Joliet's St. Joseph Hospital with telegrams and calls.

Members of the Barr family were gathered outside the intensive-care unit, waiting. Police guards stood at the door.

Inside, Bill Barr was wrapped in bandages—only his eyes and the left side of his face were visible. A tangle of tubes connected his body to plastic sacks of liquid

4

suspended above his bed. A television screen monitored his vital signs; a nurse moved silently about the room.

Three men in business suits stood over his bed: Mitchell Ware, head of the IBI; and two detectives. One man held a tape recorder and microphone.

Like everyone else, they were waiting.

Three hundred miles away, in the Veterans Hospital at Ann Arbor, Michigan, another man had suffered an explosion. It was still going on.

Quietly, inside the body of Walter Stokosa, the end of the world—his world—was close at hand. A research prosthetist, he had breathed the fumes of an experimental plastic into his lungs.

Midnight, alone: a temperature gauge on a molding oven malfunctioned. A combination of plastics intended for use in an artificial limb ignited and filled his lab with a thick black smoke.

The accident, at first, seemed minor. Walter extinguished the fire himself. But a sour taste from the smoke remained in his mouth. And inside his body, within the very microbiology of his cells, a chain reaction that threatened to end his life had begun.

In May 1970 he admitted himself to the Veterans Hospital. His fingers and toes had become numb and were beginning to curl inward on themselves.

He entered the hospital, balancing precariously on his crippled feet, his hands tucked close to his body, out of the way. Within a month he was confined to a wheelchair, the deterioration of his hands and feet accelerating.

His mind remained active, clear—filled with the ideas his hands could no longer bring into life. A research prosthetist is scientist, physician, and skilled craftsman.

5

Walter Stokosa the craftsman was dying along with his hands. The rest of him was fighting desperately to stay alive.

Each week on Thursday he crawled from his bed into a specially fitted wheelchair. Metal bars protruded from the wheel rims, allowing him to manipulate the chair himself. His hands could no longer grip the wheels.

The special chair was at his request; he did not wish to be pushed.

Thursday. He wheeled himself to the elevator and rode silently down to the second floor. His face, long practiced at showing no emotion, showed none now.

He wheeled himself down the long halls and into a physical therapy room. The Gymnasium it was called, a room of parallel bars and mats and weighted pulleys attached to the walls. It smelled of human sweat and anxiety.

Other days he came here to work against the steady deterioration of his body. On Thursday he came to watch. The outpatient amputee clinic was in session.

A hospital surgeon and two consulting prosthetists were seated at a desk near one end of the room. The amputees waited nearby, some in wheelchairs, some leaning impatiently on their crutches, some in a long row of folding chairs brought in for the clinic.

They came forward one at a time. The surgeon and the prosthetic consultants made an examination and gave their recommendations.

Walter moved his wheelchair close to the desk. But remained apart, and listened.

His face, still young for its fifty years, was intent; his eyes alert to every movement and detail. He was cleanly shaven, his gray hair neatly groomed in the flat-top style of a decade before. The hospital robe was clean and carefully arranged on his now too thin body.

As he watched and listened, he pried his gnarled hands open and closed, working them constantly against his chair and each other. Whenever the younger of the two prosthetists—a tall man in his early twenties—spoke, Walter's face became especially intent, almost critical.

This man, Jan Stokosa, was his son.

Jan (pronounced Yahn) was keenly aware that his father was watching. But it did not affect his work. It changed nothing. The critical eye of his father was inside him, always.

At twenty-four, Jan was a respected prosthetist, graduated number one in his class at Northwestern University, certified, successful. A year before he had taken over his father's business, leaving the older Stokosa full time for research.

Jan was athletic, good looking; he handled the patients quietly, good humoredly. A marked contrast to the surgeon with whom he was working.

The surgeon was an older man, impatient, moody, often raising his voice to an amputee. Each time this happened Jan would step back and stand quietly, waiting. When the storm had passed, he would approach the patient again.

Jan listened to each patient intently, his eyes and examining hands in concert with the patient's voice. He did not hesitate or recoil, not even the slightest gesture, at the clublike stump of an arm or leg. Nor was he steeled or cold to his task. He seemed to have, almost, a reverence for his work which carried over and attached itself to the patients themselves. Despite his youth, they seemed to believe in him, trust him.

But to a careful observer there was something wrong.

Something felt as much as seen: his manner, perhaps a little too professional, too perfect—controlled, totally; his concentration was uncanny, machinelike, almost inhuman.

His eyes gave the only tangible clue. A band of white was clearly visible below the iris, creating the impression that he was staring upward. Stress—prolonged, constant. An incredible force was locked inside, waiting always for the chance to be free.

It was, if one looked closely, not unlike the look in the eyes of the man in the iron chair, his father.

Bill Barr's mind was alive, yet lost, held prisoner in a maze of sedation and shock. He wandered within himself, searching for clues to who and what he might be, what had happened. . .

Delirium and time played tricks within him. In his mind he watched a cross burning; he watched from the dark window of his apartment, the flames casting strange shadows about him. Then, an accident—his car leaving the road, the sound of glass and metal raining down. . . Dark images from the past, an endless train of nightmare scenes, passed before him.

He became dimly aware of the glass and stainless steel around him, then the nurse. For an instant he was back in a post–World War II Antabuse clinic—Bill is an arrested alcoholic. He could feel the blinding shock of the Antabuse drug and alcohol mixing within his system, hear the screaming of other patients undergoing this same violent treatment. This passed, became unreal.

Finally, he saw a black face staring down at him—it was Mitchell Ware. Bill knew the face.

In the state legislature Bill had actively opposed the

formation of the IBI. "No governor should have a private police force," he had said. Strangely, he remembered that now. Mitchell Ware, the leading candidate to head up the proposed bureau, had been sent to the legislature to lobby Bill on numerous occasions—with no success. But they had developed a mutual respect, became friends. Bill blocked the formation of the bureau on three separate votes. It was finally passed. All this Bill remembered.

Reality crept through this unguarded door, began to work its way forward and back, erasing the dreams.

The puzzle took shape. He knew who he was, where he must be. He *knew* what had happened.

Dojna had warned him.

Mitchell Ware observed the beginning signs of consciousness. The tape recorder was ready. He leaned close.

"Who," he asked carefully, "who did this to you, Bill?"

"Mitch. . . ?"

"Yes, Mitchell Ware. Who, Bill? Who?"

"Dojna warned me," Bill whispered.

The tape in the recorder was turning. One of the investigators held the microphone close to Bill's mouth.

"*Who*, Bill? Who might it be?"

Bill was silent.

Mitchell Ware spoke the names of a number of suspects. The press had already listed them: the fourth Mrs. Barr, his soon to be divorced wife; the Mob; the Ku Klux Klan; several other opponents of his open-occupancy bill. A long list of names.

To each Bill whispered "No, no. . ." and shook his head very slightly, *no*. He would not believe the possibilities, could not believe. . .

Finally, Mitchell Ware was finished. He leaned close.

"Get better," he said, "get better, Bill."

Then, for a time, Bill was alone. He became more aware of his pain; it became less general. He could locate its centers: his face, his side and arms, his leg. His thoughts were becoming clearer. He remembered the explosion, snatches of lying on the driveway; his leg. . .

He felt with his hand where his right leg should be. Nothing. But his senses were not yet ready to comprehend, to realize.

The nurse was bringing in his family one by one. Each could stay only moments.

First, Tony. Bill stared at this man, his son; a slim, deeply tanned version of his own younger self. Bill had attended Tony's graduation from college in Florida only days before, their first really happy time together in years.

Bill and Tony's mother had separated when Tony was only thirteen. Tony soon was in trouble: the schools, the police. Bill had intervened, tried to help. He and Tony had argued, bitterly and often. Their relationship hardened, became distant and cold.

But gradually, finally, they had found each other again. Tony's graduation had somehow confirmed this. They had celebrated, together; a new chapter in their relationship had opened—only days before.

Bill said Tony's name, softly.

"You're going to be all right, Dad. You're gonna get better," Tony said.

Then, for a moment, Tony stood over the bed, anxious, wanting to say more. The nurse ushered him out and brought in a young woman, Robin, Bill's daughter.

Bill and Robin had always been close. Bill tried to say something, could not. Robin was crying.

A second daughter, Kathy, a teenager, had not been allowed to come to the hospital.

Bill's brother and sister were brought in. Each stood an

awkward moment and left. They had said something but Bill hadn't heard. He was drowsy.

He asked for Dojna. Then he slept.

He woke to find a strange man looking down on him. The nurse was gone. The silhouette of the policeman outside the door had disappeared. He felt strangely alone, frightened.

His heart began to pound.

"I'm here representing Mr. ————." The man gave the name of one of the area chieftains of organized crime.

Bill's vision began to blur. How? Why? He tried to scream for help, but could not.

The man continued. "Mr. ———— did not try to kill you. Mr. ———— does not try to kill people. He wishes you to know this. Do you understand?"

Bill signaled with his eyes that he did. The man left.

Bill's body was covered with sweat. He closed his eyes and listened to his heartbeat; it slowed gradually, became more normal. He fell into a light sleep, dreaming the explosion.

When he awoke, he was totally aware. The nurse was back in the room. He noticed the policeman, once again outside his door. He saw things clearly.

The last remnants of the protective haze of shock were peeling away, leaving him exposed. A new level of pain filled his senses.

The explosion played back through his mind; he could feel himself being lifted, the burning. . .

His fingers went again to his leg, felt the vacant space slowly in disbelief. He touched the bandaged remains of his thigh; his fingers recoiled, searching the vacant space below, again, and again. . .

The realization began in his stomach, like the starting of a roller coaster; he was tipping downward, slowly—then

11

a rush like the world had been ripped away, and he was
falling.

Falling. . .

2

Bill was moved to a private room, his condition stable. Policemen still stood outside his door. Visitors were not yet allowed.

He was alone.

It was two days since the bombing. Bill was weak from the physical trauma and pain of his wounds. And from the tight-lipped battle he fought within himself.

Inside he was screaming in agony and disbelief. Hopelessness and rage ebbed and flowed, sapping the little strength his body retained. He stared, not seeing. His family had been allowed into intensive care because he was expected to die. Now he must rest, conserve his energies. He was to live.

To live, with a part of him gone forever. To live. What did that mean now? What could he do? In his mind, he had already lost Dojna. Beautiful Dojna.

Bill had met her six months before at a social function; he was unable to forget her. Especially her eyes.

Dojna had dark eyes, dark eyes that accented her fine black hair and struck in bold contrast to her fair skin and delicate features. Dark eyes that had seen much—the front lines of war in Eastern Europe, the hard realities of being an immigrant in Chicago. Her eyes in an unguarded moment were deep and sad. Then in the next they would sparkle and dance, the corners of her mouth playing with a smile.

She spoke with the soft accent of her native Yugoslavia.

Dojna was mystery, and sadness, and warmth.

13

Bill had made inquiries. He learned that Dojna was a psychiatrist and chief of staff at a Chicago hospital. He called, asked to see her again.

Bill was already separated, his divorce in process. But Dojna was attuned to the mores of Eastern Europe, not the United States. She refused.

Bill persisted. Finally she agreed to see him *with* a chaperon. With a chaperon Bill conducted his courtship.

Their relationship grew quickly. Despite Dojna's reluctance. Despite the ever-present chaperon. They agreed to be married.

In the spring of 1970 Dojna asked Bill to hire a bodyguard. She had become uneasy about the violent opposition to his open-occupancy bill; she had seen the danger in several statewide investigations he was conducting. But he was unable to conceive that his enemies would go so far as to harm him physically. He refused.

Dojna's warning went unheeded.

Then, June 2, the bombing, his leg was gone. *Everything* was gone. All that had been, so quickly gone. The future before him was faceless.

Bill held onto himself tightly. He hated the past for promising so much; he feared the future—endless space, vacant, dark. It pulled at him with a gravity force. His face showed the strain of holding against it.

And then he could hold no more. An impulse surged; he tore back the sheet that covered him. He faced the bandaged stump, and the empty space below.

He began to weep. The wild falling began within him again. This time he knew he could not stop it. He called out for Dojna. And then he was tumbling downward, screaming inside, weeping.

For two hours, he fell deeper and deeper into the emotions of panic, and rage, and despair, losing all hold on himself and the earth. Two hours; he endured forever, in the subjective time of the mind. Nightmare faces of chaos and death screamed and laughed around him; they beckoned him to join them in madness—*had not his world been cruel and unjust*. But something within him held.

At last he lay at this journey's end. He was wet with perspiration and his own tears. He was exhausted beyond anything he had ever known. But he was ready to fight.

Somehow, he was now ready to fight for his life.

The next few days were filled with visitors: family, friends, and politicians—the great and the small.

Special tables were set up to accommodate the constant arrival of flowers, each bouquet carefully inspected by the police guards.

Adlai Stevenson Jr. was pressing the state legislature for a dynamite-control bill. Governor Ogilvie was pressing the IBI for action. Local police manned two twenty-four-hour hotlines, asking for any information related to the Barr bombing. Bill's family offered a reward.

In the midst of this whirlwind Dojna arrived. She had been doggedly working her way through the red tape of both the hospital and the police. She was neither relation nor celebrity. It had taken time.

She brought a special salve for the scars she knew must cover Bill's face. He looked away as she applied it gently around his eyes. He could not look at her.

"Your leg?" she asked. "Is that why you won't look at me?"

Bill was silent a long time. Finally, he answered.

"Not the leg really," he said. "I think I'll learn to get along without that. I didn't feel like it at first, but. . ." he paused, "it's you I'm going to have trouble getting along without."

15

She stopped applying the salve. "I don't understand," she said.

"I'm not holding you, Dojna. You agreed to marry a *whole* man. That's all changed now. . .no one can blame you."

Dojna's eyes were hurt, almost angry. "Do you really think my love is so shallow?" she said.

"It will *be* there, Dojna. Always. You'd have to look at it, live with it."

"Bill," she said. "Bill don't. . .don't tell me what I could look at. . .no, don't use me as your excuse. If you want to back out, if *you* no longer want *me*, say so, but don't use me this way."

Bill was silent.

"Well," Dojna said, "do you want me?"

Bill nodded his head.

Dojna began to cry, very softly. "Bill, I'm glad," she said. She started to rub the salve gently around his eyes once more. This time he did not look away. The future now had a face.

But around that face everything was still uncertain. And the uncertainty was now somehow worse. Willing to fight, he had allowed the future to become real. Now it was much more than real. It was alive and important.

John J. Houlihan walked down the hospital corridor toward Bill's room. His walk made a special sound that Bill recognized, long before Houlihan appeared at the door. In his mind, Bill could see him coming.

John Houlihan lifted his artificial leg by hand and pushed it forward with each step. He wore a broad smile, his blue eyes looking always ahead. He never looked down toward his leg, as if he paid little mind to the inconvenience he suffered—the message was plain: you could pay little mind to it too.

Houlihan's smile filled the doorway. Clearly, it was not sympathy he brought. He turned to the policeman on duty. "I'll not be shooting him, Harry: I've not even brought my gun. But I'll be closing the door here—as soon as this fine nurse leaves us. Go on now," he said cheerfully, "it's all right."

The policeman grinned and closed the door behind the departing nurse. Houlihan turned and surveyed Bill carefully.

John Houlihan and Bill had served together in the state legislature. They had stood at the same mill gates shaking hands on winter mornings. They had supported and opposed each other with equal enthusiasm on the floor of the legislature. Bill, a Republican, had once contributed heavily to Democrat Houlihan's financially troubled campaign. They were friends.

"I've been thinking about you," said Houlihan. "Today, in fact. I was looking at the statue of your father in the capitol—an imposing man, that one. . .but you've made your own place in the world, Bill, and there's those of us who know it."

After returning from World War II Bill had shunned the opportunities afforded the son of State Senator Dick Barr. He took a job as a door-to-door examiner in the Federal Rent Control office in Kankakee, Illinois. During the next nine years he was promoted six times to become the national director of the Office of Rent Control in Washington, reporting directly to President Truman. He was given the Arthur Fleming Award as the outstanding young man in the federal government.

When the Office of Rent Control was discontinued in 1953, Bill began his first in a series of business ventures, and by the early 1960s he was a millionaire in his own right.

In 1967 he returned to Illinois with his own name, and his own money. He was elected to the state legislature and in his first term was voted outstanding freshman legislator by his colleagues.

"Yup," said Houlihan, watching Bill closely, "you could have had it on a platter but you made your own way—it took spunk to do that. And the way you beat the booze. . .I fought the booze myself, ya know. No easy battle, that one. No sir." Houlihan looked off a moment, as if remembering. "Well, I was thinking like this and I knew you'd be fine—you've been in a battle before."

Houlihan moved slowly to one of the chairs beside Bill's bed, moving his leg with his hand, looking always ahead, smiling. He lifted his prosthesis and balanced on one foot, gripping the arm of the chair with his free hand. Slowly he lowered himself into the seat.

"Did I tell ya I heard Tony's speech?"

Tony had been a constant visitor. Bill, sensing Tony's desire to do something for him, had asked Tony to stand in at a scheduled speaking engagement. Tony, a few days out of college and never having given a speech in his life, agreed.

"The boy did a fine job, Bill; you'd have been proud. He talked about you, ya know. . .said you'd always been a father to him, stood by him, said to keep your space in the world open—you'd be back! Got a standing ovation, he did."

Bill looked thoughtful. Houlihan noticed, went on. "I talked to him some, after. He's a strong-minded boy, Bill. I suppose you two have had your battles. . .but he loves ya, that's sure. Oh, they're a trial aren't they—I've a dozen of my own, ya know."

18

Houlihan lifted himself from the chair with his arms. He got to his feet.

"Bill, I'm going to show you something. It's not pretty but you'll know my reason." He took down his slacks, exposing a wooden prosthesis strapped and fitted from above his waist; it was stark, the metal joint at the knee stared like the eye of an alien being. But Bill was not repelled. He found, instead, that he was intensely interested.

"No stump," Houlihan said simply. "I've got to sit in this bucket here." He patted the stiff girdle that surrounded his pelvis. "And it hurts some, there's no denying it. But I do everything short of running I've a mind to." He was suddenly serious. "I went eleven years after Bougainville with nothing but crutches. They didn't know how to fit a man with no stump. . .I was twenty-one years old, Bill." John Houlihan was silent for a moment, looking back to the war and his own struggle. Then he was upbeat, smiling.

"But they're doing wonderful things these days," he said. "I talked to the doctor, Bill. You've got a decent stump for them to work with. It's not the end of anything, no matter what it feels like now." He pulled up his slacks. "They're even making them pretty. Not like this antique of mine here." He grinned broadly.

"Now I know you've got things to think about, and I've got the business of the good people of Illinois to tend to. I'll be seeing you soon."

Looking ahead, John J. Houlihan walked out the door, lifting his leg with a hand and pushing it forward on each step. Bill listened to the uneven sound of Houlihan's walk, as it faded away.

Bill felt as if they had had a long conversation but couldn't remember having said a word himself. Bill

19

smiled. Houlihan had played him like an instrument—he'd been had. Bill's smile broadened. It wasn't opening night for the act either, Houlihan had done it before. Bill sensed this—he was a politician too. But none of this mattered. The message was real.

Before the sound of Houlihan's walk had faded in the hallway, Bill knew what he was going to do.

He *knew* what he was going to do! A future was beginning to take shape in his mind.

3

Walter Stokosa had admitted himself to the hospital. He also made the decision to go home.

He instructed his wife to wrap a pencil thick with masking tape, until it would fit in his crippled hand. With this instrument he sketched a stairlike apparatus that would enable him to lift himself in and out of his wheelchair.

The sketch was crude, but carefully done. The pipe from which the apparatus was to be constructed was drawn in great detail; the joining elbows in correct perspective, creating an accurate three-dimensional view. Draftsman's arrows enclosed the measurements. One-half-inch galvanized pipe was specified in large childlike letters near the bottom of the page, the initials W.S. scribbled below.

Walter gave the sketch to Jan and told him when to have it completed.

He made the necessary arrangements for his release from the hospital.

He was ready.

But in the process he had needed the assistance of his wife and son. At fifty years of age Walter Stokosa was grudgingly learning that no man is an island. Always before, he had been able to avoid this realization.

Always before. . .

Walter grew up in the gray inner city of Detroit. As a young man with no high school diploma, he found himself locked into a series of menial jobs. Each one the same as the last, each one focusing more clearly on the confining walls that seemed to surround him.

Roller skating was his first means of transcending this environment. And the first confirmation of his unyielding belief in himself.

Walter began skating at the age of seventeen. He joined a figure-skating club and soon began to compete. Every day he rose at 4 A.M. and practiced two hours before going to work at Detroit's Fisher Body plant; each night he practiced until the roller rinks closed. It was 1937.

Two years later, at nineteen, he won the Senior Men's National Figure Skating Title. Still employed at the factory, he sponsored himself in more competition, often riding a train all Sunday night to be back on his job Monday morning. He won the coveted Hurst Trophy in New York's Madison Square Garden. He successfully defended his national championship in 1940 and was invited to represent the United States at an international competition to be held in Germany.

But the war was approaching and the State Department disallowed the trip. Soon he was drafted.

The army put Walter to welding. His skating at least temporarily at an end, he turned his full energies to acquiring this new skill. He practiced and learned with the same fanatic dedication that in a few short years had made him a national skating champion.

His skill grew quickly and drew him a steady diet of tough assignments. He performed these with great satisfaction, enjoying his status as a skilled tradesman, absorbed in the work. But the war ended and Walter left welding behind with the army.

Shortly thereafter he married. Son Jan was born in 1946 to be followed soon by a daughter. Walter worked for a time as a skating instructor in Denver. But the pay was insufficient to support his growing family. Competition offered no prize money. He was unable to find work as a welder, his lack of formal education blocking his entry to this skilled trade.

In early 1949 he returned with his family to Detroit, and the factory. The walls of his life were closing in once more.

Twenty years later, crippled, perhaps dying, Walter must surely have thought back to this time when the future had defaulted on so much so quickly.

Walter sat quietly in his wheelchair. Jan watched, nearby. They were in the Stokosa home. Walter would face the future here. The doctors had admitted there was nothing they could do. Walter's condition was unique. The doctors could not even predict the next development, or if he would live. It was now mid-June 1970.

Walter sat facing the stairlike apparatus Jan had constructed, preparing himself.

The frustration with his gnarled body did not show in his face. Nor did his constant fear that the cell deterioration within him would soon affect his mind. His face was composed, but not calm. His composure was an act of supreme self-control, not acceptance, not resignation, not even the slightest adjustment to his condition.

Walter Stokosa was at war. From deep within himself he directed the battle, relying on his own intelligence and will. Already he had asked for two things, but he wanted no help. Not from God or his fellow man. He wanted to stand alone.

This had always been so.

In 1949, after the promise of being a national skating champion, after becoming a highly skilled welder in the military, Walter was back in a Detroit factory; this time at the Chrysler Motor plant, his ability and ambition once more frustrated.

A chance comment set him free.

Walter overheard a man say he was looking for a welder, a highly skilled welder, to do some delicate work in orthotics. A few days later Walter began welding braces part time for Kaufman Orthotic Appliances.

John Kaufman, the owner, recognized Walter's ability and offered him more work. Within a year he was training Walter in all aspects of the making and fitting of orthotic appliances.

Walter kept his job at Chrysler, working the afternoon shift. Every morning he went to the orthotics shop at eight and worked a full day before starting his shift at the factory. In spare moments he read medical textbooks and orthotic journals. His appetite for learning was insatiable.

As with roller skating and welding, orthotics became his life. He had found another means of expressing the incredible force that lived within him. That it was orthotics he pursued was coincidental. His real pursuit, as it had always been, was perfection.

At the end of two years John Kaufman announced to Walter there was nothing more he could teach him. He suggested prosthetics as a more challenging field; he felt Walter could find full pay for his talents in this work.

John Kaufman was instrumental in securing an apprenticeship for Walter at the E.H. Rowley Co. Walter quit work at Chrysler and at the age of thirty-one began his training in prosthetics.

He worked during the day at E.H. Rowley and attended school at night. A high school diploma was first. Then he began the necessary courses to become a certified prosthetist.

Six years later, in 1956, Walter Stokosa was certified by the American Board of Certification in Prosthetics. He left E. H. Rowley and took a new position with Wright and Fillipis Inc., an orthotics and prosthetics chain. He was soon advanced to the position of consulting prosthetist.

During the next ten years, he would establish and direct the orthotics and prosthetics department at the University of Michigan in Ann Arbor. And then move on to his own practice, and ultimately independent research.

And then the accident: the midnight fire with its deadly smoke, unleashing chaos inside his body.

Jan watched his father force his hands onto the iron frame of the transfer stand. He had built it exactly to Walter's specifications; he watched with a technician's eye, assessing the suitability of his work. That this was his father did not intrude on his observations. Since his childhood, he had been trained to screen out such interference.

Walter lowered himself awkwardly, step by step, to the floor—repositioning his hands with great difficulty at each plateau. It was strenuous and painful. But his face showed nothing.

Once on the floor he forced his body into a strenuous routine of stretching and rocking exercises. Jan talked with him as he lay resting between periods of exertion. They discussed business, patient by patient, the technical details of each case.

Jan's father struggled on the floor before him, yet Jan remained strangely aloof, detached. He sat, composed, in a straightbacked chair nearby, his hands folded loosely on his lap. He did not have to fight the natural impulse to help. It wasn't there.

Anxiety, if anything, was less than usual. For the first time in Jan's memory the threat of physical violence between them was not present.

At the age of seven Jan had begun his training as a prosthetist. While Walter served his apprenticeship at E. H. Rowley and completed his courses in night school, Jan was schooled also.

Jan was trained rigorously in anatomy. He was forced to learn the physical properties of woods and glues and a variety of metals and plastics. On weekends he spent both Saturday and Sunday with his father, working, learning.

Walter was a hard master, impatient, often losing his temper, beating Jan for missed lessons. He drove, pushed, tried to create in Jan the perfection he endlessly sought in himself. Jan was to be his ultimate creation.

Walter's personal success seemed only to deepen his desire for perfection in Jan. He drove him ruthlessly, attemped to control him completely. Walter's temper grew ever more volatile.

On a winter afternoon he beat Jan's dog, King, a Siberian husky, to death with a rod. The dog had growled at Walter.

Eleven-year-old Jan watched: the rod struck again and again, a brilliant red stain spreading across the new snow, Jan's dog twisting and growling in pain, eliminating his bowels into the pooling blood. The struggle subsided, King lay in convulsions, growing ever more quiet. And still the rod fell, methodically, brutally—his father's face twisted with rage. These images would live always within Jan's mind.

And after, his father washing his boots, slowly, carefully—without a word.

Jan hated him. And feared him. The dog had been somehow a lesson, a thing he was supposed to see. The price of disobedience, perhaps. Jan was growing older. Threats and childhood beatings might no longer suffice to control him. Or, perhaps Jan and the dog had become too close, threatening Walter's ability to involve Jan totally in prosthetics. Perhaps it was both. Walter Stokosa did very little, even in the heat of temper, without a purpose.

But whatever the case, it was not necessary. The reservoir of feelings Jan held for his father ran deep, far deeper than the surface layers of hate and fear.

Walter infected his son with the quest for perfection. Already Jan worshipped at this altar. Already he viewed as shallow and unworthy those who lacked his father's zeal. Here Walter was supreme. Here Jan loved and respected him. A powerful bond had grown between them, a tapestry of dark colors, deeply woven with their shared quest for perfection—their god.

By the age of thirteen Jan would independently construct his first artificial limb. At sixteen he would be able to diagnose and prescribe a prosthesis.

And this had been only the beginning.

By the time of Walter's accident, at twenty-four years old, Jan was respected and secure in his profession. His future promised much, perhaps greatness. But at what price. . .

Jan watched his father crawl back up the iron frame and lift himself into his wheelchair. Jan's face was impassive, a reflection of Walter's.

They had discussed patients, nothing more. Walter had questioned Jan in great detail about each case. Jan had answered in turn, describing exactly what he was prescribing, the level of progress. . .Their discussion had been polite, technical, exact.

27

But now, Walter was uneasy. Jan wanted to leave but somehow knew Walter wished him to stay. He sensed that Walter was making a decision.

Emotion crept into Walter's face—a look Jan had never seen. Jan felt, within himself, a surge of emotion, as though he were somehow experiencing Walter's own hidden fear and pain. But Jan's face revealed nothing; he pushed these feelings back, and back, until they were only shadows, lost, somewhere within him.

"Jan," Walter said, "Jan, my mind is totally intact."

Jan nodded.

"There's still a great deal I can do with my mind. You've got to talk with me, Jan, really talk with me. You have ideas for research. Share them with me. Tell me what you're thinking about, let me help you. . .let me give you my ideas. You've got to use my mind, Jan, you've got to be my hands."

Walter grew quiet, composed himself, straightened his clothes.

Jan felt only a small part of Walter's plea. Walter himself had trained Jan to ignore such things, to push them aside and keep his eye on the target. Unknowing, Jan did this now. It would be years before he understood the full magnitude of the words he had just heard.

He let the door of Walter's prison slam shut—"Sure," he said blandly, "we can talk."

But they never did. Jan never gave this. And Walter never asked again.

4

June 19, 1970, seventeen days after the bombing, Bill Barr was wheeled down the hospital corridors to the St. Joseph Hospital auditorium. Police bodyguards walked briskly beside him. Photographers formed a moving knot outside the security. Bill smiled frequently, saying hello to the many photographers he knew.

Just outside the auditorium, John Houlihan was standing. The wheelchair was stopped while Bill and he shook hands. Cameras flashed.

Inside, the reporters were waiting. Television cameras were set up in the aisles and at the back of the auditorium. A table with a dozen microphones was waiting in front. Bill was wheeled up and turned to face the assembled press.

"Gentlemen and ladies," Bill said, looking out at the reporters, "I have some announcements to make. But I know you have some questions of your own and want to take some pictures. So let's get that out of the way first."

The cameras began.

Bill wore a black and white houndstooth robe with a red silk lining. The scars on his face were evident, although Dojna's constant application of salve had already done much to heal them. Bill leaned back and waited for the cameras to stop. This was not his first press conference.

The questions began.

"Mr. Barr, who do you think is responsible for the bombing?"

"I'm afraid I don't know."

"Several papers have reported the possibility that it was organized crime—in response to your refusal to cooperate in recent mob activities in Joliet. Is this a possibility?"

"I have no reason to believe this," Bill said.

"Mr. Barr, there is speculation that the recent conclusion of your divorce was a move to take away your former wife's motive and prevent a second attempt on your life. Is this true?"

Two days before, Bill had taken a private ambulance to the county building in Joliet to finalize his divorce. It was granted to him on the grounds of mental cruelty, ending months of speculation and gossip, and ending for his ex-wife any possibility of financial gain in the event of his death.

The press, of course, had followed. It had turned into a circus: cameras and questions. Speculative articles, with pictures of Bill arriving in the ambulance at the courthouse, had filled the Chicago area papers.

"Although I can understand this line of speculation," Bill said, "let me say this: I have no information which leads me to believe my former wife was involved in the bombing in any way."

"What about the Ku Klux Klan? Is it true that they threatened. . ."

Bill cut in. "Gentlemen, I've told you I have no idea who did this to me. I'm not even sure I want to know. The police and the IBI are handling the investigation. My sights are set on the future—I'll not dwell on this unfortunate moment in my life."

"Will you have a bodyguard after leaving the hospital?"

"That will be up to the police." Bill paused. "I've been

thinking about getting one of those remote control starters for my car though. I am getting a little touchy about *that*."

There was laughter, releasing tension and bringing Bill closer to his audience. When it subsided, he continued to speak. "I'd like to make my announcement now. There have long been rumors, and at times newspaper stories, to the effect that I was dissatisfied with my work in the state legislature." Bill looked sternly out at the group. "I'm sure none of you ever wrote any such thing." There was scattered laughter. Most of the reporters smiled. So did Bill. "It has been reported that the pace of the legislature is too slow for my 'flamboyant' personality, and that I am frustrated by protocol and party loyalties. My Republican colleagues, as you know, have even accused me of being a Democrat. It has been rumored that I would seek a political position where I would have more personal power and freedom to act, where I could more directly affect things on a day-to-day basis. I'd like to deal with this speculation once and for all—it's absolutely true. This coming election, I will seek the office of mayor, right here in Joliet."

Several questions and a current of conversation among the reporters began all at once. Bill lit a cigarette.

Two hours later he was wheeled from the room.

He was smiling. And as one reporter put it—"looking like a winner."

The days in the hospital brought Bill closer to his children. Emotions are not guarded in the presence of tragedy. A strong feeling of family was building between them. They were all growing closer to each other, and to Dojna. That Kathy, his second daughter, had not been allowed to come was bothering Bill much more than it would have a short time before.

31

Robin, who lived in Joliet, had invited Dojna to stay with her, to be closer to the hospital and Bill. The two women turned to each other for comfort and strength. And the visible bond between them was, in turn, a source of strength to Bill.

When Bill told Robin that he and Dojna were to be married, she was quietly pleased. She put her arms around his neck and wished him happiness.

Tony had only begun to know Dojna. Still, Bill could see they liked each other. And this, of course, pleased him.

In a strange way, Bill felt lucky. His personal life had never been so satisfying. Dojna and his children were so close to each other and to him, as if the bombing had broken down barriers in all of them, especially him. They were like pieces of a puzzle, fitting together. And within himself, he could not even name what had changed.

Before, telling Tony about the marriage would have been an ordeal. Now it was different. Bill trusted Tony to understand, to believe him. Perhaps because Bill believed himself.

They were alone in Bill's room. Bill sat on the edge of his bed, his crutches lying beside him. He wore a blue silk robe over the regular white hospital pants and gown. His right pantleg was pinned up neatly behind him. Tony sat in a chair nearby, his stockinged feet resting on the bed beside Bill.

Bill was looking intently at Tony. "How are you, son?" he asked.

"Fine, I guess. What do you mean?"

"There's been so much emphasis on me. I just wanted to know how you're doing. . .what your plans are? We never did get to talk about that down in Florida."

Tony was quiet. An undercurrent of caring had always

been there between them, holding their relationship together, despite all the problems they had had. But this caring was now on the surface, in perspective. Perhaps for the first time.

Tony felt this. And the feeling was heightened by the fact that it came in the midst of Bill's own personal tragedy. It was a great deal of change to absorb so quickly.

Several minutes had passed since Bill spoke, but the silence had been easy.

"I'm going to travel for a while, Dad. My friends and I want to parachute in some different parts of the country." Tony was an accomplished skydiver, belonging to the elite group that had logged over a hundred jumps.

Bill nodded his head. "And then?"

"I don't know, get a job I guess, in Florida—keep jumping."

"This skydiving, it's not just a hobby, it's important to you, isn't it?"

Tony nodded.

"What kind of job will you get?"

"I don't know. I have to think about that. . . I'm just not sure, right now."

"Ever think about politics? Houlihan says you gave one hell of a speech the other night."

"No politics," Tony said. "That's your thing, not mine."

"All right," Bill said.

There was another comfortable silence.

"Tony," Bill said, "I've been married four times—you know that."

Tony nodded.

"Well, I'm going to get married again. . .to Dojna."

"All right," Tony said.

"Now, with my track record this is going to be hard to believe, but this time it's going to be different."

33

Tony smiled. "I thought I was the one who always said that."

Bill smiled with him. "I guess we've both said it more than our share." Bill paused, became serious. "Tony, it's like when I finally quit drinking. Even though I'd said I would quit a hundred times before, I *knew* when I meant it. This is like that. I *know* this is going to work."

Tony nodded his head.

"And, Tony, I'd like you to stand up with me, be my best man. . .would you do that for me?"

"Yes, Dad," Tony said softly. "I'd like that."

Rehabilitation in the hospital proceeded quickly. Bill had begun learning to walk on crutches during the second week of his stay. Whirlpool baths and general exercise were the only other prescribed activity. The real work would begin later, after Bill had been fitted with a prosthesis.

Bill had questioned the hospital constantly about "getting a leg." Finally, the surgeon who had performed the amputation sent a man from a prosthetics firm around to see him.

After further consultation with the hospital doctors, it was decided Bill would go to the Chicago Rehabilitation Institute to have his prosthesis prescribed and to learn to walk. The firm the surgeon had recommended would build the prosthesis.

Bill was in a hurry. He could sit, stand, and navigate stairs on his crutches. He learned quickly. The physical therapy people cautioned him constantly to slow down. But it did no good.

Also, he was turning their facility into an office, talking politics or business while he took his exercise. Often, hospital personnel had to wade through a group of people to speak with him.

Bill had a nice way of bending the rules. The physical therapy people liked him. But clearly, it was time for him to go.

The hospital administration was also ready. Bill was costing them an extra person on the switchboard. His mail was burying the main desk. The press conference had been an ordeal. And this appeared to be only the beginning.

Bill's energy was back and he was shifting into high gear. Fortunately, along with his spirit, his body was healing in record time.

On June 25, just twenty-three days after the bombing, Bill Barr was released from the hospital. The next day he and Dojna were married in a quiet ceremony at his Black Road apartment. Tony and Robin were beside them.

Bill stood on his crutches during the ceremony. His own determination and the warmth from Dojna and his children made the future seem bright, made him totally optimistic about what might lie ahead.

Late June 1970.

Walter Stokosa laid his newspaper on the table before him. He turned the pages with his knuckles, impatiently—looking for something.

He stopped. His face tightened, hiding the surge of emotion within him. The article he had hoped *not* to see was there. The headline, in large black letters, read:

JUDO VICTORY HAS STOKOSA IN NATIONALS

Jan had taken up judo shortly after high school. He had progressed quickly, placing in minor tournaments and winning several YMCA titles. But a series of knee injuries and subsequent surgery had forced him periodically from competition. Layoffs of up to a year at a time would cool his interest and bring Jan's full energies back to prosthetics. When his knee was healed, he would begin again to compete. Walter had watched this cycle closely, fearing judo as a rival to prosthetics.

Just before Walter's accident Jan had achieved his longest injury-free period of competition. He had won twenty consecutive victories, and was double-promoted from middle-degree brown belt to black. He won the Amateur Athletic Union title for the state of Michigan and competed successfully in the Midwestern Regional Championship.

He was nationally ranked and an Olympic contender.

Walter's accident did not turn Jan back. If anything he turned more completely in the direction of judo and away from prosthetics.

Jan arose at four each morning to exercise before going to work. He left work early each afternoon and ran ten miles before dinner. Evenings he practiced at the local YMCA. Weekends he traveled to tournaments.

Jan's brother-in-law, also a certified prosthetist, had come into the business and was taking over much of the work, as Jan devoted himself more and more to judo.

Walter was in no position to argue. Earlier he would have undoubtedly made a stand. Now he could only watch.

Surely, through his own experience with skating, he must have recognized that Jan was attempting to escape—escape the environment that he, Walter, had so carefully constructed and controlled.

36

Surely Walter knew this, as surely as Jan did not.

They sat in a long line in a hallway, waiting. They sat on folding chairs along one wall or in wheelchairs or they stood on crutches. Some surrounded by family and friends. Some alone. Men and women and children, all different shapes and sizes, but each with an arm or a leg missing; one man, both legs; another, only his hand. . .

The hallway itself had once been pale green but had been washed with strong soap until it was now almost colorless.

Bill Barr's tailored clothes looked, at first, out of place in this line. But he did belong here, his crutches and the pinned-up leg of his trousers said so. "Millionaire or pauper, this is the best place," the doctors at the hospital had said, "to have a prosthesis prescribed."

Bill sat on one of the folding chairs, fidgeting with his appointment slip. Dojna sat quietly on one side of him; his bodyguard sat, expressionless, on the other. Tony, in jeans and open-necked shirt, leaned against the opposite wall.

At the end of the hall was a desk and a few wooden chairs. A consulting surgeon and a physical therapist were seeing the amputees, one by one. All conversation with the doctor could be overheard the entire length of the hallway.

There was an anxious silence among the waiting.

This was the outpatient amputee clinic at the Chicago Rehabilitation Institute. It was June 29, 1970.

Finally it was Bill's turn. The physical therapist unpinned his pantleg and pushed it up, exposing the unbandaged stump of his leg. The surgeon felt of the stump with his hands, speaking, at first, only to the physical therapist: it was healing well, there was no infection.

The surgeon stepped back and eyed Bill's stump critically.

"Why haven't you been wrapping your leg?" he said.

"I beg your pardon."

"You haven't been wrapping your leg."

"I don't know what you're talking about."

"They told you about it in the hospital."

"No they didn't."

"Well, you've got to wrap it before I can do anything." The surgeon nodded toward the physical therapist. "Mrs. Cameron will show you how. You'll come back here on this day in two weeks. Then we can see about a prosthesis." The surgeon poked at the stump. "Any phantom pains? Can you feel your foot?"

"A little," Bill said. "Sometimes it feels like my toes are curled up and I can't get them down."

"This is quite normal," the surgeon said. "It's a psychological phenomenon. Doesn't sound like you have it bad at all. When it occurs you simply have to outthink it. Your toes are not there. Concentrate on that."

The physical therapist took Bill off into a small room and showed him how to wrap his stump with an elastic bandage. Wrapping is done to aid circulation and to begin the process of stabilizing and shaping the stump: a series of tight wraps near the end, followed by a crisscross of looser wraps higher up. Through this process, the flesh is forced to stabilize into the approximate shape of a cone. This is prerequisite to wearing a prosthesis. The physical therapist explained this while she demonstrated the wrapping. And she talked about phantom pain.

"If the phantom pains get to bothering you," she said, "rub the scars on your stump." She winked at Bill. "That sometimes stops them, at least for a while. Usually they stop altogether in a month or two."

"Thanks," Bill said.

Mrs. Cameron finished demonstrating the wrap. "There," she said, "got it?"

"I believe so."

"Good. Do it every night, and keep it on all you can during the day. Tighten it up when it gets loose. We'll see you back in two weeks." She left the room.

Bill stood for a long moment staring at the elastic bandage.

The drive home was silent. Bill and Dojna sat in the back seat, the bodyguard and Tony in front. Tony drove.

At the Black Road apartments they pulled past the carport, still ragged and torn from the explosion. Bill stared out through the car window at the splintered boards and twisted metal.

"Will somebody call my office and tell them to get that damn thing fixed!"

No one said anything or looked at Bill for several seconds. It seemed longer. Finally, Tony spoke. "Sure, Dad," he said, "I'll take care of it."

Tony parked the car, a dark blue Cadillac, identical, except for color, to the one destroyed in the bombing. He parked it directly outside the apartment. They all sat quietly for a moment after the engine had died.

"I'm sorry I snapped," Bill said.

Tony waved it away with his hand. "Dad, forget it."

In the hallway, outside Bill's apartment, there were several reporters. A police guard stood by his door. Bill smiled and exchanged greetings with the reporters. Tony and Dojna did not smile or say anything. They stood back, suspicious, not liking the reporters. Bill was used to this; Dojna and Tony were not.

"When will you have the prosthesis?" one of the reporters asked.

"Not for at least several weeks," Bill said.

"Why the delay, Bill? I thought it was supposed to be sooner."

"Off the record, or on?" Bill asked.

"Off."

"The hospital screwed up, some hocus-pocus with an elastic bandage they forgot about—or didn't know about."

"On the record?"

"My leg is healing beautifully. There was a preliminary examination today, the prosthesis will be prescribed in two weeks. I expect to be walking shortly after that."

"Any progress on solving the bombing?"

"Ask the IBI."

"When will you start campaigning?"

"I'm campaigning right now, I expect to be able to count on all of your votes." Bill smiled. "It's been a long day, boys, you'll have to excuse us. Thank you."

The reporters stepped back, allowing them to pass.

Inside the apartment they settled, exhausted, into chairs in the living room.

"I wish I knew more about this leg business," said Dojna. "This clinic. . ." she shook her head. . ."not to mention the hospital."

"They're supposed to be the best," Bill said.

"I know," said Dojna, "I know. . ."

"Maybe they're just overcrowded right now," said Tony. "I think it was the place, more than anything."

Bill nodded his head. "What the hell," he said, "it's only two weeks. Come on, let's get out of this mood. Why don't I take us all out to dinner? I'll call Robin. . ."

The following two weeks were filled with a multitude of minor setbacks and victories. Bill had to learn to plan everything three steps in advance: the shower, the toilet, the simple procedure of getting dressed—a lifetime of things he had taken for granted now had to be planned and carefully executed. Impatient, by nature, Bill constantly found himself with his hands full at the wrong time or in a place too small to turn around with his crutches.

Bill's family closed ranks and became his strength. They ate dinner together at the Black Road apartment, almost nightly, and sat talking into the evening. He was constantly surrounded by warmth and support.

The entire family became expert at wrapping Bill's stump, although no one, it seemed, had much luck with keeping it tight; the elastic bandage was forever slipping off and having to be rewrapped.

Tony chauffered Bill, and provided him with a willing set of legs. Serving as liaison to Bill's office, he became a vital personal link in much of the day-to-day operation of Bill's land development and real estate business.

During this two-week period Bill scheduled and attended his first political meeting of the mayoral campaign. On crutches he went to the home of a political supporter for a coffee klatch with neighborhood voters. There was also the political business at the capital to attend to: Bill was still a state representative. He spent long hours on the telephone and once traveled to Springfield for a crucial vote.

Although he was busy, these two weeks seemed long. Bill was anxious to get a prosthesis, to walk.

Finally the waiting was over. He returned to the amputee clinic at the Chicago Rehabilitation Institute and was given a prescription, a requirement in the state of Illinois, to have a prosthesis constructed.

5

The prosthetics firm was an unpleasant surprise, at best. Bill had expected to visit a modern medical facility. But he found instead a dingy, commercial building in a run-down section of town.

The waiting room was dirty and small. Discarded newspapers and some coverless magazines were piled on a low coffee table. A few badly worn chairs sat against the walls. The doors were not even hinged to accommodate handicapped persons.

A large number of people were waiting.

Inside was a long hallway with three or four tiny examining and fitting rooms off each side. A handrail extended the full length of the hallway. At its end was a work area where some half-dozen technicians built prosthetic and orthotic devices.

The work area resembled, in miniature, a high school woodshop: all benches and tools and a few large machines—a band saw, a drill press, a lathe. And noise, and too many people.

The smells of glue and sawdust and oil, mixed with the predominant odor of human perspiration from the examining rooms, filled the hallway.

Bill was escorted by a woman to one of the examining rooms. An old man was being taught how to walk on his prosthesis in the hallway by a man in a white coat. The old man hung on to the rail with one hand and took small, unsure steps. There was not enough room for Bill to get by on his crutches. He and the woman had to wait until the old man reached the end of the railing before they could travel the hallway.

Inside the room Bill stood in a turnstile while a man wrapped his stump with a plaster bandage. The rolls of bandage were taken from a bucket of water and wound and smoothed over his stump; this was the mold from which the upper part of his prosthesis would be made. A number of measurements were taken and written on a chart with Bill's name.

After about ten minutes the plaster mold was removed. The man told Bill he should return in three weeks for an initial fitting. In about six weeks he would have his leg.

Bill did not want to wait. He had money and influence and was willing to pay the price not to.

But first he called one of the doctors at the hospital and reported the conditions at the prosthetics firm; he questioned if this was the right place to have his prosthesis built? He was told that these were "leg makers," not doctors; that their place of business was a factory, not a hospital; that he was expecting too much—*this was the best place.*

Bill recontacted the firm and arranged for his initial fitting to be done under the supervision of the surgeon at the Chicago Rehabilitation Institute—in a week and a half. He would have the finished leg in three.

On August 1 Bill received his leg.

It was made of wood with a free-swinging hinge at the knee. The hinge had to be locked and unlocked with the motion of each step, creating a pause each time the knee reached the full-lock position beneath him: a toy-soldier walk. A solid-piece-construction rubber foot was attached to the leg and fitted inside a conventional shoe.

The leg was held in place with a *total-contact* vacuum.

44

The stump was inserted into a socket, constructed from the initial plaster mold of the stump. A small metal valve regulated the pressure, ensuring the socket's suction grip on the stump. There were no straps or belts.

This was Bill's leg—as prescribed and approved by the consulting surgeon at the Chicago Rehabilitation Institute, and built by the prosthetics firm recommended by the surgeon who had performed Bill's amputation.

The owner of the prosthetics firm informed Bill that he need not go elsewhere to learn to walk, they could teach him there. But Bill stuck to his original plan and returned to the Chicago Rehabilitation Institute.

Within four weeks he could walk unassisted—he left the Chicago Rehabilitation Institute for the last time.

He had fallen and sworn, gotten up, and fallen again. He had showed up unscheduled to practice, and refused to sit down when told. But he learned very quickly.

In less than half the expected time he had completed his training. A slight discoloration had begun in his stump. Bill was told this was normal. No one seemed concerned.

There was some pain when he walked, but he had expected this. He was more than willing to trade a little pain for the mobility he had gained. He was happy.

Bill decided to take Dojna on a honeymoon. The election was still months off. They would fly to Miami and pick up Bill's boat. From there they would go on to the Bahamas.

Tony saw them off on the plane, and then began to organize his own skydiving trip. He could leave Joliet now.

Everything was fine.

Bill and Dojna were proving the critics wrong. Their

marriage was working. Adversity had brought them close, very quickly. Perhaps closer, more quickly, than could have ever been achieved under ideal conditions.

Bill was not even experiencing the bouts with impotency quite common to lower-extremity amputees.

The trip to the Bahamas, although several months late, was truly to be a celebration of their marriage.

Bill had begun boating years before on the Potomac, during his Washington days. In 1967 he had purchased a fifty-five-foot Hatteras yacht off the display floor at the Miami boat show. It had three staterooms, a living room, dining room, and galley, all fully air-conditioned. It had been specially outfitted by the manufacturer for the boat show. It had everything.

The above-deck lines were sleek in white Fiberglas, the hardware bright and shining in the Florida sun.

Dojna fell in love with the boat; it was a dream.

Bill skippered the boat from Miami to Lucaya on Grand Bahama Island himself. No crew. He managed the ladders between the flying bridge and the engine rooms slowly but quite well. Having the prosthesis was a great freedom after two months on crutches.

The seas on the way over were calm, green, and beautiful.

Bill docked the boat expertly in Lucaya's harbor. The dockmaster stood alongside watching.

"Hey, Barr," he shouted. "I heard they tried to kill you."

"It was all in fun, Eddie," Bill said.

"I heard you lost a leg."

"It's true," Bill said, tapping his prosthesis. "But I've got a wood one, supposed to be better than the original."

"That right? Hey, what the hell are you doing on this boat with no crew?"

46

"Honeymoon, Eddie. Don't ask so damn many questions; get the lines."

"Okay, Boss, okay. But you're crazy as hell, still crazy as hell."

Bill and Dojna lived on the boat during the day and played on the island at night. They ate in the many fine restaurants, they gambled in the casinos—they even danced.

Bill seemed to know everyone. Not just the wealthy residents and the staffs of the hotels and casinos, but the poorer people they passed on the streets as well.

"Did you live here?" Dojna asked.

"Almost," Bill said.

They were on the sundeck of the boat. Dojna was drinking Dubonnet, Bill his habitual ginger ale. A painting Dojna had begun was on an easel nearby.

"Almost?" Dojna questioned.

"Back in the early fifties," Bill began, "I had a ninety-nine-year lease on a big chunk of this place—grew cucumbers and tomatoes. Sold them to the chains on the mainland when Florida got hit by a frost. Was gonna make big money. . ."

"And?"

"Complications, problems. . ."

"Tell me."

"Bahamians wouldn't work. Didn't matter what you'd pay them. I had to negotiate a deal and import Tahitians, flew in with them on an old cargo plane myself."

"And?"

"Couldn't use the market facilities on the mainland, had to build my own."

"Sounds expensive."

"It was. I had to pull together a syndicate of investors. Damn near lost my shirt."

47

"Damn near," Dojna said, looking around at the yacht.

"Well, I did manage to eke out a small profit."

They both laughed.

"What happened?" she asked.

"I sold out to some limey who thought he was going to build luxury hotels and casinos down here. He wanted my lease and my Tahitians. Crazy idea. I told him it would never work."

They laughed again.

Dojna was learning about this man she had married and about how much there was about him to learn, and Bill was learning about her too. And they were happy.

On the return trip to Miami they were caught in a storm.

Bill had checked the weather carefully, delaying their departure twice. He was confident of his ability to handle the boat, but feared his lack of agility between bridge and engine rooms in bad weather. Also, he had been experiencing increased pain in his stump during their final days on the island, and wanted to avoid a long turn on the bridge.

They left Lucaya harbor in clear weather with mild to moderate seas. Two hours out ten- to twelve-foot breakers were rolling over the front of the boat. The seas came up suddenly without a corresponding change in weather, creating the eerie sensation of being in two worlds at the same time. Sailors in the Gulf area are familiar with this "bathtub effect" in the waters. Bill had seen this happen before. But Dojna was new to the sea, and was terrified.

She stood on the bridge, wanting to be close to Bill. He explained their situation to her carefully and calmly. They were in a following sea. *Broaching* was the only real danger, but all they had to do was run with the waves, keep their course—and they would be home free. Bill did not tell Dojna about what might happen if they had engine trouble. He listened alone to the steady drone of the engines, rehearsing constantly what must be done if one faltered.

Five hours out they hit the foul weather that was creating the seas. It turned cold and began to rain. The wind sprayed the upper decks with water.

For fifteen hours, Bill stood on the bridge, expertly keeping the boat in tune with the seas. His voice remained steady and calm. He talked to Dojna about the sea, explaining, teaching—helping her focus outside herself and stay calm.

She listened and learned. And stayed calm. But it was Bill's voice itself, more than anything said, that she clung to.

Finally, safe in the Miami harbor, Dojna realized she had, again, seen a new aspect of her husband. And he of her.

They were exhausted, but happy, and very much together.

Back in Joliet, the mayoral campaign heated up. Bill heated it up. He met the voters at factory gates and supermarkets in the morning, spoke to businessmen over lunch, and did two coffee klatches each evening. Joliet stood in the shadow of Chicago and had never really developed mass media of its own. Campaigning was door to door, one on one.

And winter came early that year. From mid-November on there was snow. Bill was learning to walk, quite literally, on ice, with his new prosthesis.

Bill brought his open-occupancy fight to the center of the mayoral campaign. He attacked the city fathers for ignoring the problems of Joliet's poor, and he pushed cronyism in local government out into the open, exposing questionable no-interest bank accounts established with city money.

He returned his bodyguards to the police and the IBI, stating that he refused to live in fear.

Many political observers were holding their breath. The echoes of the June bombing had hardly died away.

In the mayoral primary in January, Bill defeated the incumbent mayor and a field of nine other candidates. He carried the black districts in Joliet by a larger percentage than John F. Kennedy had in 1960. But the campaign had really just started. The regular election was still ahead. And the conservative forces in Joliet were now ready to take Bill Barr seriously, very seriously.

An investigative reporter was brought in from Chicago to look for skeletons in the Barr closet. And to shake them.

Bill's leg, since his return from the Bahamas, had become steadily worse. It was giving him a great deal of pain. At the end of each day, his stump was plum colored and too sore to touch.

Dojna, as a medical student, had been exposed to the surgical procedures and treatment of amputations and, very briefly, to prosthetics. But this had been years before, and her practice in psychiatry had taken her far from this area of medicine. Dojna knew enough to know that something was wrong, and that she was not qualified to deal with it. She urged Bill to see a doctor. But he was in the midst of a campaign.

A month later the pain had intensified. Bill began having trouble sleeping at night. His eyes became bloodshot and the hollows beneath them began to darken. Finally, he took Dojna's advice.

The surgeon who had performed the amputation had

subsequently retired and moved to Florida. Another doctor was recommended.

Bill's stump was examined.

He was told there was nothing wrong. The discoloration was normal during the adjustment period—nothing to worry about. A certain amount of pain was to be expected. He was given two prescriptions: one for sleeping pills and another for medicine to clear up his eyes.

Bill resumed his campaign. And the pain grew worse. It was almost unbearable, especially at night.

Bill woke in a cold sweat. He had been sleeping only a short while. For a moment he didn't know where he was. When it was. First he thought he was in the hospital, after the bombing. Then his Joliet apartment and the mayoral campaign he was waging swam into focus.

He realized he was holding his stump with both hands, rocking slowly back and forth in his bed. The general ache in his stump had become a throbbing pain that spread upward into his lower back. The scars on the end of his stump, where the remains of his leg had been brought together, burned intensely. For an instant Bill panicked, for an instant it seemed unbearable and he started to rise up to run. Prolonged pain will do that—give a person the crazy impulse to run. Even when you've got only one leg.

Bill looked at the clock. It was almost morning. The pain was not as hard to manage in the daytime. The whirl of the campaign helped him to put it aside.

But the nights, the nights were getting damned hard to get through. And he was already taking too many sleeping pills. He knew that.

Things had looked so good at first. Bill thought back, trying to understand.

But Bill could not understand. And his leg grew steadily worse.

By April 1971, the month of the mayoral election, he was finding traces of blood in his prosthesis at night—and sweating through three sets of pajamas before morning.

6

Jan woke with a start. It was the middle of the night. The phone was ringing.

The voice was his mother's. She sounded tired and far away, but her message was totally urgent. "Come over here, quickly," was all she said.

Jan dressed and ran from his apartment into the Michigan winter night. It had not snowed since he came in. The windshield of his Corvette was clear. The door made a hollow sound in the cold air when he slammed it behind him; the motor made an ungodly roar. Everything seemed exaggerated and incredibly clear, like seeing and hearing for the first time.

The streets were almost empty. Jan drove very fast. He handled the gears expertly, making his way quickly through the side streets onto the main road. The lights of the occasional cars he passed blinked in the rearview mirror, and were gone. But there was no hint of recklessness. There was no emotion in his driving at all.

Jan's face was controlled. He did not allow himself to think; he only drove.

The street where his parents lived was not well lighted. Jan could see flashing red and blue lights of police cars and an ambulance from a long way off. Then, all at once, it seemed, he was there. The comforting noise of the engine was gone. And he was stepping into the cold.

Two men were carrying a stretcher down the steps from the front door. A sheet was draped over it. As Jan came up the walk an arm, *Walter's arm*, flopped out from under the sheet and hung limply; it bounced roughly with the steps of the two men who carried the stretcher. The sheet slid down on the body.

Jan looked fully into his father's face as the stretcher passed.

He felt nothing.

So that was death. Yes, that was death quite clearly. There was no mistake. Death was very easy to recognize, especially when it was your own father.

Jan found himself thinking of the kittens he had drowned as a boy. There had been too many kittens. Walter had made him hold them in his hands, submerged in a bucket of water. Jan remembered the incredible strength of the kittens as they drowned, the explosion of biting and scratching—the raw strength of a thing so small. And he had held his face impassive, as Walter had taught him. He remembered the fading of the strength and the sudden limpness within his hands. That was death. He knew what death was.

He watched them load Walter into the ambulance, tucking the arm back under the sheet. Yes, that was death. Walter was dead.

Then the doors of the ambulance closed. Jan remembered Walter standing beside him when he fitted his first prosthesis. He remembered, and felt fully, the immense pride Walter had not been able to hide. And he began to cry. For the first time since he was a very small child, Jan cried.

Grief and a sense of incredible loss swept over him. This was followed almost immediately by a feeling of great relief. Jan took a deep breath: Walter was dead.

He looked up at his mother standing in the doorway. She was also looking at the doors of the ambulance. And in her eyes Jan saw them too, the oscillating emotions of relief and grief.

She had taken Jan and his sister and left Walter, many times, always to return. Jan could see, in his mind's eye, his sister and himself being ushered quickly into the family car, suitcases being hurriedly loaded; Jan could feel the fear, even now, that his father would come unexpectedly home and catch them...and he could feel, as he had felt it then, the inevitability of their return.

His mother had always, in the final analysis, stood by Walter. She had acted as a buffer, trying to protect Jan when Walter was angry; she had salved Jan's wounds when Walter had beaten him, and she had soothed him. But always, in the end, she stood by Walter, speaking his praises, and telling Jan that all the minor wrongs could be forgiven, for in things of importance Walter's judgment and skill were supreme.

Jan looked at her now and realized how little he really knew her, and how little he knew of the bond that had held her and Walter together. She was crying, but she also breathed very deeply.

Walter was dead.

It was February 3, 1971.

The funeral was not for three days. On each of these days Jan sat in the funeral home with his father.

At first he stood beside the casket. After a time he sat in a chair, very near. Later he would find himself sitting further and further away, withdrawing gradually to the back of the room. Each place he sat gave him a different view of Walter's body.

For the first time in his life Jan felt he could talk with his father. There was so much of Walter's teaching that Jan believed in. But the points where he did not agree, often minor points, had always kept them apart. Any point of divergence, however small, had always triggered Walter's temper. And these points had always existed. Walter had taught Jan to observe and analyze better than he had taught him to obey. So always there were differences, and conversation between them often ended in anger, incredible anger.

Now Jan felt he could talk freely, tell him how much he loved and respected him—and how much he hated him. And why.

But the task was too great. There were so many things to say, and such a short time for them to be together. It would take a lifetime to sort it all out. Within himself, each word Jan spoke to his father led him off into memories, away from his purpose.

Jan remembered a prosthesis about which he and Walter had disagreed, he remembered their discussion in detail—and then Walter suddenly reaching for an iron bar from a bench nearby and screaming for Jan to leave before he killed him. Jan could see in his mind the totally controlled, glasslike features of Walter's face suddenly twisting and burning out of control. Jan was seventeen years old.

That same day Jan returned to his home late in the evening. The kitchen was covered with blood where Walter had beat his fists against the cabinet doors. A large living room chair had been thrown through the screened-in porch. Walter sat in a rocker, passed out. A bottle of bourbon, three quarters gone, lay in his lap. His bloody hands gripped a shotgun. It was loaded and cocked.

Jan removed the gun from Walter's hands, unloaded it, and laid it back. He went to a cabinet and collected the remaining shells for the gun, and went to bed.

In the morning Walter was repairing the porch screen

with a coil of brass wire, making each square a perfect copy of the one before it; his face was serene. Neither he nor Jan ever mentioned the night before. They simply went back to work.

Always, they went back to work. They made people walk. Walter had said it just like that, many times—*they made people walk.* It wasn't a vocation, it was a religion. And it bound them.

Why? Jan found himself suddenly returned to the present, asking, Why?. . . Why had Walter been like this? Was it the depression, the war? What had *his* father done to him?

And then he knew this would not be so easy. Walter was dead. But Jan was not free. Not yet. Not just like that. It was not so simple as just telling Walter how things would be, where they agreed and where they disagreed, where they would stand together and where they would not. They were *bound.* Jan was suddenly confused and frightened.

Were he and Walter inseparable? Was he to *become* Walter—in spite of anything he might do? "Already I have your glass face," he said to the body in the casket before him. "I don't know how to *feel,* I can't *feel.*"

Jan wanted to run, run from Walter. He needed distance, a great deal of distance. And time. It was not *time* for this. Not yet. He was too close to it, too close to Walter.

Jan brought a photographer into the funeral home late that night. Against the wishes of the funeral director, he had Walter's body photographed. He had pictures taken from all different angles. Later, when he was ready, he would want to begin here—to sort things out, once and for all.

Perhaps Jan needed proof that Walter *was* dead—proof for all time that Walter Stokosa could really have died.

57

The funeral itself was a blur. Jan sat next to his mother and sister, but he was not with them. He was not really there at all. Within himself, he had already left.

The final stretch of the mayoral campaign turned ugly. Bill's image as a swinger, his previous divorces, his bout with alcoholism, were all dragged before the public eye. The investigation of the bombing was presented as an unfair financial burden to the city of Joliet—the consequence of having the flamboyant Mr. Barr for a citizen. And Dojna was called a bride of political convenience.

Oddly, talk of Bill's father—who had once been mayor of Joliet, and gone on to become a state senator and political "boss" of Illinois—was injected into the campaign. The public was warned against "a return to the arbitrary politics of the rich and powerful."

The predictable mudslinging was not new or particularly troublesome to Bill. He had heard it before in other campaigns, he expected it. But the introduction of his father was a new angle. It was an ironic twist to have his father injected back into his life at this time.

Bill had grown up as "Dick Barr's kid." When he was fourteen the legal driving age in Illinois was lowered to fourteen. It was raised back to sixteen two years later. As a teenager in the middle of the depression he had driven a new Cadillac around Joliet.

While in college, political opponents of his father burned down a house where Bill was attending a party. The headlines began—SENATOR'S SON...

Strange scars, these: the psychological impressions of unrestrained power and affluence at a time when people around him were worrying about having enough to eat (as a boy Bill had helped his "across the tracks" friends steal from the Barr kitchen).

And the hatred from people he did not even know: hatred that was really for his father, a man he saw only through a screen of servants—a man he did not even know.

Bill had spent the first part of his life overcoming this handicap—a handicap made worse by the fact that most people saw it as an advantage.

It was ironic to have all this dredged up at this time: the old handicap alongside the new.

By election day Bill's face was thin and had a yellowish, waxen hue. The pain in his leg was constant, he could sleep for only minutes at a time. And the political barrage against him was unrelenting.

Dojna was drawn and tired, also. She was working hard herself, setting up a new psychiatric practice in Joliet, as well as trying to follow Bill through a sixteen-hour day of campaigning—and trying to fill all the special needs the loss of his leg had created at home. Both as a doctor and as a wife she felt the need to be able to quiet his pain, but knew full well she could not.

And Dojna was new to politics. She was horrified by the personal assaults on Bill. At times she felt as if she had been thrown back into the days just after the bombing, when every newspaper and radio was blaring Bill's name.

She sat alone with Bill at his campaign headquarters when he received the election news. He had lost.

Bill put down the phone and took a deep breath. He did not have to say it, Dojna knew from his face.

"Bill," she said, "I'm sorry."

Bill shook his head—"It's all right," he said. "I half expected it, half wanted it—how in the hell would I be mayor, right now, anyway."

Dojna was silent.

"It's over," Bill said, as if to convince himself, "I lost." He looked at Dojna. "We've got to put this campaign behind us. It's hurt a great deal, I know. But it's just politics. People don't mean the things they've said. You've got to believe that, Dojna. It's over now. . . I think we put on a damn good campaign. . ."

"I liked the speeches to the high school students," Dojna said.

Bill smiled, thinking back. "I'm afraid that was dumb," he said, "and perhaps self-indulgent. They can't vote, and it's the wrong time to court youth—anything they like, their parents don't."

"The sermons at the black churches, they were very good—and the people loved you."

Bill smiled again. "It's the same thing," he said. "They were going to vote for me anyway. I should have been spending my time downtown. . ."

Bill paused, suddenly serious. "You know," he said, "I didn't put on such a good campaign at all. I put on a hard campaign. And long. But no good. I needed the crowds too much, I didn't think enough about votes."

"Bill. . ."

"No, Dojna, what I say is true. I had a big lead and I lost it. I made mistakes. . .lots of mistakes."

"You've been in a lot of pain."

Bill shrugged. "Lame excuse," he said, and tried to smile.

"Bill, don't. Pain is a powerful thing. You expect too much from yourself."

"Well, I finished it, at least. I guess I am proud of that."

"I'm proud of you."

They sat quietly for a moment.

"Just two more things to be done," Bill said. "I've got

to talk to my campaign people, and then we've got to go over and congratulate the new mayor. Then we can go home."

It was late on the same evening. The speech to his campaign workers had been made. The new mayor had been publicly congratulated. The campaign was slipping away and Bill was finally turning his attention to himself.

Dojna found him sitting alone in their living room. She turned on a lamp and sat down beside him. She waited for him to speak.

"Dojna, I've got to do something about the pain. . ."

"The new prosthesis?"

During the campaign, through conversations with other amputees, Bill had uncovered what might be the cause of his pain. His stump could be going through a prolonged adjustment period, changing size and shape—perhaps because of such early and heavy use, perhaps because it had not been wrapped during the first weeks after the amputation. If this was the case his stump was being alternately bound too tight, which would cut off the circulation of blood, and then being given too much freedom, which would allow it to hammer down against the bottom of the prosthetic socket with each step.

"It makes sense," Bill said, "and I don't really know what else to do—that doctor I went to was no help."

"Maybe another doctor. . ."

"Let's try the leg first."

"All right," Dojna said, "I'll make the appointment."

This was April 20, 1971.

The next morning Bill was at his office. By noon he knew he was in trouble. He had totally neglected his business during the latter part of the campaign. Things

61

had slid badly. And the coming recession was making itself felt in the building industry.

Bill sat at his desk and stared out the window. If he could just free himself of the pain, get on his feet—everything would all seem so much more possible.

7

Jan sat at the desk in his father's office. It was late at night. A small lamp was burning.

The desk was covered with papers, boxes of supplies were piled along the wall; an experimental plastic leg that Walter and Jan had been working on lay on a corner of the desk.

Jan picked up the leg and turned it slowly in his hands. He began to think about a possible variation on the design, then quickly put it aside.

The next morning he would leave for Japan. There he planned to continue his training in judo. The United States Olympic team was his goal.

Jan's brother-in-law, also a prosthetist, was to run the Stokosa prosthetics practice; it was needed to support Jan's mother and sister. Jan had spent the last three months, since Walter's death, readying his brother-in-law to take over—Jan did not plan to return.

He sat for several hours in the office that night, not really thinking, not understanding why he was there, and not feeling the need to understand.

A page had been turned in his life. His plan to travel to Japan and study judo was written at the top of the next. The remainder was blank. He sat and stared at the blankness, absorbing it. Was this freedom? He wondered.

Finally he got up and turned out the lamp. He walked slowly out of the office. He walked in the dark, out through the casting room into the hall, out of this building he knew so well.

Bill was back in the same crowded little room, waiting. He had come to be fitted for a new prosthesis.

A week before he had met with the prosthetics firm representative, the same man who had seen him in the hospital after the bombing. It was agreed that a new leg would be made. *Technically,* the old leg would be repaired—Bill had no medical prescription to have a second one made.

The prosthetist confirmed Bill's hypothesis as "reasonable" and "worth a try." He confided to Bill that, in his opinion, surgeons knew very little about prosthetics anyway, and Bill was better off dealing directly with the firm. He suggested a "piston knee" in place of the "old-fashioned" hinge in Bill's present leg, a thing, he said, which should have been prescribed in the first place.

Bill's stump was to be recast and the total-contact socket remade. This would provide an automatic adjustment to any changes of size and shape the stump had undergone. Also, the piston knee would make Bill's walk smoother; he would no longer have to lock the hinge on each step, his stump would be relieved of the minor but continuous jolting this created.

Bill was hopeful; he wanted, *needed,* this new leg to work. But he could not shut out the feeling that he had been through all this before—and it hadn't worked.

He glanced around the waiting room at the other amputees, guessing he could pick out those here for the first time. They looked surprised, as he had been, at the rundown appearance and crowding. He wished he knew what to tell them. But he had no answers himself.

Maybe he should be trying something else? Maybe another doctor—did that make more sense? Maybe. . . Bill tried to push these thoughts from his mind as he waited.

Finally he was called.

The hallway and the smells from the work area were the same. The tiny fitting and examining room was identical to the one he had first visited.

His stump was wrapped with wet plaster tape—exactly as before.

The technician left, promising to return shortly. Bill stood, a bright light in his eyes, waiting for the plaster to dry. His stump was throbbing, sending sharp pains up into his hip and lower back. The burning in the scar tissue was being intensified by the irritation from the drying plaster. He unconsciously bit at his lower lip.

In three weeks he would have the new leg. He resolved within himself as he stood there waiting that the new leg *would* work.

Three weeks; he would hang onto that.

Jan found a small apartment about forty miles from Tokyo and settled into a routine.

He rose each day at 4:30 A.M. and ran five miles into the Japanese countryside. It was springtime, and the air was cool. The country road he ran on was usually deserted; it wound gently into the foothills of a small mountain.

Each morning he stopped at a spring that surfaced not far from the road. He drank and rested and watched the sun rise.

Several times he tried to think about himself and Walter and what he might ultimately do. But there was an almost tangible barrier, a closed door in his mind that would not come open. Whenever he tried to see into himself or see more than the immediate future, this barrier was there.

Invariably he found himself concentrating totally on his immediate goal—the Olympics. Judo had become his entire world. Within it his life made sense.

The run back to his apartment ended with a quarter-mile sprint—and puzzled looks from his now stirring Japanese neighbors.

After a shower and breakfast, he took the monorail into Tokyo: to the Kodokan. The Kodokan was a center for judo—the most famous, perhaps the finest, *dojo* (training place) in the world.

Jan arrived at the Kodokan by nine each morning. After a brief warm-up in the exercise area he would attend one of the many classes, always in session.

Entrance to a class was gained by kneeling quietly nearby. Soon the ranking member of the class would notice and offer an invitation to join. Permission to leave a class was gained in a similar manner.

The classes were not ongoing or organized, in the American sense. People simply gathered together in groups of similar rank, the highest-ranking member in charge. Instruction and the opportunity to practice throwing techniques and holds were mutually exchanged.

Rigid personal discipline and absolute adherence to routine were required in the classes. A great deal, both mentally and physically, was expected; only serious students were welcome at the Kodokan. The respect, however, for those who could demonstrate ability and dedication was complete; it crossed national lines easily. Jan was well pleased with the classes.

As a black belt, Jan was expected to exchange his skill and knowledge with others; at his level, at the Kodokan, the idea of just receiving instruction was alien. Jan did not speak Japanese. But this was not looked on as a barrier; judo can be easily taught with the language of the body. Skill was what mattered. Here again, Jan was deeply impressed with the rigid fairness of those around him. He began to understand more fully the philosophical roots which had initially attracted him so strongly to judo. The *mokuso* meditation, when the class knelt together in silence at the end of each session, began to take on a new and deeper meaning.

In addition to the classes, Jan spent at least some time each day in the area of the Kodokan set aside for *free practice*. This was a large open mat where black belts engaged in a controlled competition, just short of combat. Here, no invitation to practice could be refused. Jan was often approached by black belts of much greater weight and experience. According to custom, he would bow and utter "onegai shimasu," the Japanese words for "please instruct me."

The lessons were often harsh.

By midafternoon Jan was at Tokyo's Waseda University to practice with its intercollegiate team. This was allowed on the strength of a letter of introduction from Dr. Sachio Ashida, a sixth-degree black belt and Jan's former coach in the United States.

Unlike the Kodokan, the atmosphere at Waseda was totally competitive, even nationalistic. Several members of the Waseda team were leading contenders for the Japanese Olympic team. Some did not like the idea of helping to train their competition.

Practice was, by any standards, long and grueling—sometimes brutal.

Several evenings each week Jan spent at a *dojo* near his apartment. Here, as at the Kodokan, he both gave and received instruction.

Jan's life was Spartan. He became hard and keen, beyond anything he had previously achieved. Even his apartment reflected this attitude. He cooked simple meals on a hot plate and slept on a hard mat. The shower was outdoors with cold water only.

And he was alone. His relationship with the Japanese people was formal, correct—nothing more. But this was as he wished it to be. There was no room within him for people.

He stayed to his schedule, focusing his concentration ever more completely upon judo. His personal discipline was unbending. He lived to excel.

But something was missing. He felt this as an endless ache in his chest—*something was missing*.

In early May 1971 Bill received his new prosthesis. The "piston knee" was a noticeable improvement: it was physically easier to operate and resulted in a smoother, quicker walk. But there was no change in the level of pain.

He tried the leg for several weeks, wanting desperately for it to work—but the pain remained, as constant and excruciating as before.

It had been almost a year since the bombing. And for almost seven months of that time Bill had lived with this pain, twenty-four hours a day, every day—there was no relief.

The campaign had provided an external focus that he now did not have. He had used the campaign to delay the realization that. . .what? His leg had not healed properly? His prosthesis was wrong? What? All he knew was the pain. The campaign had served as a dam, holding back reality.

But the campaign was over. Quickly he had set up another dam—the second prosthesis; he had used this in a similar way. And this too had collapsed.

Bill now returned to the doctor he had previously seen. His stump was again examined—but the doctor only prescribed more sleeping pills, he could find nothing wrong.

The long-delayed reality of his situation was rushing in on him. He was badly crippled, in constant pain, and *no one seemed to know what to do.*

"I can't remember anymore when it didn't hurt—it's all blurred together."

Dojna and Bill sat together in a Joliet restaurant. Bill found he could manage his pain better in public; it forced him to a level of self-control he was finding difficult to achieve at home.

"Maybe it's crazy," Bill said, "but it's true, I can't remember ever being all right—it's like thinking about someone else, someone I knew a long time ago, not myself. It scares me."

"I've made the appointment with Dr. Bain," Dojna said. "He's awfully well thought of. . .maybe he'll know what to do."

"It's like this nightmare I'm in is the only real thing, anything else seems like a lie. . .it seems so hopeless."

"Bill, don't talk like that. You've got to believe we're going to find the answer, you've *got* to believe that." Dojna was almost crying. She pressed her lips hard together, fighting for control of her emotions.

Bill nodded his head, fearing he might lose control of his voice if he spoke. He looked into Dojna's eyes and nodded his head—it was all he could do.

Dr. Bain was a surgeon with a reputation for innovation; he was used by a number of hospitals on difficult cases.

Dojna had learned about him through one of her medical colleagues.

Dr. Bain prescribed cortisone treatments, a series of injections given directly into Bill's stump. The injections dulled the pain, at first. But the effect wore off quickly, and each shot seemed to have less effect than the last.

Bill spent more and more time inside the apartment. He took sleeping pills in the morning to extend the period of semi-consciousness he spent in bed. The pills distorted time, more than anything; they allowed him to drift through the agonizing hours as if a much shorter interval had passed; and they made the future seem less real, less immediate. But the pain in his stump remained, and he was nauseated much of the time from the pills.

He found himself sitting for hours in front of the television, not knowing or caring what he watched—just staring vacantly at the light and listening to the hypnotic drone of the voices.

There was alcohol in the apartment, and more than once Bill stood and stared at the bottles.

At his office Bill was constantly reminded of his growing inability to use his mind. He often had to be told things several times, and on his worst days he could read a single memo endlessly and not grasp its meaning.

The better days only served to substantiate his anxiety about the state of his business. Bill's organization had always been him: his ability to perceive relationships and to make decisions and to sell—it was not set up to function without him. It was floundering badly.

Bill was still an extremely wealthy man, but his wealth was a large system that had to grow and change to survive. It was deeply interwoven with his organization. On his land and his apartment complexes and condominiums and subdivisions, there were mortgages as well as titles and deeds. The system could fall, *would* fall, back in on itself if not managed properly.

The question was only how long?

But even this did not rally Bill. The reserves of his will were being worn away, freeing the pain to affect him totally.

After several weeks Dr. Bain pronounced the cortisone treatments a failure. He observed that Bill was deeply depressed and referred him to a psychiatrist. Perhaps the pain was psychosomatic.

8

Summer 1971. Bill was placed on Elavil—an antidepressant drug. He drove twice a week to Chicago to see a psychiatrist.

Dojna was convinced that Bill's pain was not psychosomatic, but felt professionally restrained from rendering an opinion; she was too close, could not be objective. She knew this.

Again things appeared for her in awkward juxtaposition, her husband alongside her profession. And again, as with the surgical and prosthetic aspects of Bill's case, she herself could not treat him—even here, in her own field of specialty. Psychiatrist or wife: she had to choose. And of course she did—the only choice she could make.

But the inevitability of her choice did not lessen her special anguish; it did not change the human irony of being a doctor in the presence of pain in someone you love—and being kept, however wisely, from acting. It did not change this at all.

The drug, as well as the psychotherapy sessions, had negligible effects upon Bill. His pain and depression continued unchecked.

Near the end of summer the Chicago psychiatrist announced that he believed Bill's pain was not psychosomatic. He bade Bill good-bye and wished him good luck. That was all.

Bill and Dojna began to visit a series of doctors, having their hopes raised and then dashed, as each doctor failed in his effort to help. And with each failure, they found it harder to hope. They were physically and emotionally exhausted.

But they continued to search.

They sat silently in the outer office of Dr. Harold Mead, a prominent Chicago surgeon. Their faces were composed, their energies gathered.

A receptionist showed them into a large executive office. Dr. Mead was seated behind his desk. He seemed very businesslike, but not cold.

Dojna told Dr. Mead their story. He listened without interrupting.

Bill found himself encouraged, and the man had not even spoken. Bill sensed competence. It was in the doctor's face and the way he moved his hands, in the way he sat. Bill had seen these traits before, in certain men in business and politics.

Dojna finished speaking. Dr. Mead gave a short smile that was not really a smile at all; it was almost a grimace, but not unfriendly.

"Mr. and Mrs. Barr," he said, "you are obviously intelligent people. Let me be frank," he looked directly at Bill, "the source of your pain is either in your body or your mind or your prosthesis, or in some combination of these." He paused, a man who organized his thoughts carefully before he spoke. "You have had your prosthesis rebuilt, you have consulted with a psychiatrist, you have visited a number of doctors. So, where does that leave us? Back at the beginning, I'm afraid. Worse, actually. Everyone has tampered, you are deeply—understandably—depressed. My job is made very difficult." He shook his head.

There was an uncomfortable silence. Dr. Mead continued: "I will assume for the moment the problem is not in your mind, I have no reason to believe it is. If the

73

problem is in your prosthesis, I can't help you, I am not a prosthetist. The firm you have dealt with is well thought of, I could recommend none better."

"Have you ever visited their facility?" Bill asked.

"No," said the doctor. "You see, Mr. Barr, your problem lies at an unfortunate crossroad. There are prosthetics, physical therapy, and medicine—we have excluded for the moment psychiatry—and your problem lies where these intersect. Of course, the doctor prescribes to the prosthetist and the physical therapist—but how much does he actually know? You've been to medical school, Mrs. Barr, how much were you taught about prosthetics?"

Dojna was silent.

"I myself," he continued, "don't really know a damn thing about that leg you're wearing. This total-contact principle is fairly new, I can't even keep up with my own area." He paused. "But then this isn't helping you—I only want you to understand where we start. I don't wish to be the source of false hope."

"This *is* hope of sorts," Bill said. "It's the closest I've come to understanding the problem—you're the first one who's made any sense of it at all."

Dr. Mead made his strange smile. "I'm afraid, Mr. Barr, I don't see that as much help. You need relief from pain, not speculation about why you're not getting it."

"Honesty can be a form of relief in itself," Dojna said.

Dr. Mead made his smile again—"I'll leave that to you psychiatrists, Dr. Barr, and stick to what I *know*."

"May I ask a question?" Bill said.

"Of course," said Dr. Mead, "you understand that I'm charging you for this chat."

Bill smiled to himself. Honesty *was* a tonic of sorts. He found himself liking Dr. Mead.

"Your question?"

74

"Why me?" asked Bill. "Other amputees seem to get along all right—some of them have been in explosions. What's *different* about my case?"

"You make an interesting assumption, Mr. Barr" —smiling again. "Other amputees don't have problems?" He shook his head. "I'm afraid we tend to think, here, only in terms of a highly visible minority. We *see* the especially good adjustments tap dancing on television; we read about the amazing things *certain* amputees do; we hear heartwarming stories from our friends—and most of them probably are true. But what percentage of all amputees does this constitute, does anyone know? How many amputees have poor adjustments? How many are wandering from doctor to doctor like yourself, or have given up, does anyone know?" Dr. Mead looked at Dojna, then back at Bill.

"No, Mr. Barr, you've drawn a conclusion—like many people—from dramatic but insufficient evidence. All too common an error, I'm afraid. My experience tells me perhaps twenty percent of all amputees are in a situation similar to yours."

Bill had more questions, many more. But he was overwhelmed for the moment.

"Where does this leave us?" Dojna asked.

"With less than one chance in three that I can help you. . .but, if you'd like, I'll have a look at the leg." He made his strange smile with the corners of his mouth, held it a moment—"But another time I'm afraid, we've used up this appointment and there are people waiting. Make an appointment with the girl at the desk if you wish."

Dr. Mead rose and shook hands with Bill and Dojna.

They made the appointment.

Dr. Mead examined Bill's stump the following week. He diagnosed a circulation problem.

Bill's stump was covered with a great many scars. The close proximity of the dynamite had created a particularly traumatic wound—and the attending surgeon chose to clean and piece together the remains of Bill's thigh, rather than cut higher up; he had saved as much of the leg as possible. Dr. Mead felt that the unusually large number of scars which had resulted were impeding circulation and causing Bill's pain: blood was being pumped into the stump faster than it could return, creating pressure.

Dr. Mead suggested plastic surgery. He would make one large scar of the many little ones. This would create a main circuit for blood circulation, eliminating the hundreds of side roads and dead ends.

Dr. Mead stressed that this was speculation. It might work, it might not. He felt it worth the try.

The surgery was scheduled for the early fall of 1971.

Jan's final practice at Waseda University began like all the others. A gong was struck several times in quick succession. By the time the reverberations had died away all were in position on the mats, ready to begin.

There were over an hour of grueling calisthenics and a series of drills—everyone in pairs, throwing each other with a variety of techniques, no one offering resistance.

Next, the instructors and highest-ranking team members took their positions on the mats. The remainder of the group formed into short lines facing them. Free practice, the heart of each session, would fill the rest of the day.

The ranking black belt in attendance would signal the end of practice with a single note from the gong.

This day a high-ranking visiting instructor was in attendance. Jan had been warned by a Waseda team member to be wary of him—he did not like Americans.

Jan stood opposite one of the regular instructors.

Free practice ran very long. Jan, earlier in the day, had already practiced hard at the Kodokan. He was tired, ready for practice to be over. But it wore on.

Several times he imagined he saw the visiting instructor watching him. He sensed the length of the practice was intended to punish him specifically, to demonstrate his weakness. Jan redoubled his efforts on the mats.

The visitor smiled at Jan. He was a large man, nearly as tall as Jan and heavier by twenty pounds. His name was Obayashi San, a sixth-degree black belt. The smile was clearly for Jan. There was no mistake. Obayashi maintained it for several seconds. It was a smile without humor or warmth, a knowing smile.

Jan felt a psychological net being cast about him. And tightening slowly. A great similarity and an even greater difference between his father and Obayashi played through Jan's mind. But he could not hold this impression. It vanished as quickly as it had come.

Finally Obayashi pointed at Jan and motioned him out onto the mats. Within the strict etiquette of judo there was no way to refuse.

Obayashi bowed and uttered the Japanese phrase "onegai shimasu." And smiled.

Jan bowed and returned the words, his face intent.

The first fall was Jan's, cleanly. Obayashi struck the mat hard but rose quickly, no longer smiling. The room grew quiet. They gripped each other and circled. Jan felt Obayashi's leg wrapping around his own; he pulled quickly free but was tripped to the mat—a cold feeling of dread passed briefly through him. The second fall was Obayashi's, but not cleanly.

Judo is a feudal art, brought forward from actual combat into sport. The rules reflect this heritage. Obayashi had not thrown Jan cleanly. He must therefore follow him to the mat and attempt to gain submission through a stranglehold or a pin.

Jan rolled quickly but Obayashi was on him. For several long minutes Jan bridged and held Obayashi's arm away from his throat. Jan was younger and stronger than his opponent, but he was becoming exhausted. And Obayashi was skillful and far more experienced.

With a sudden effort, Jan broke Obayashi's grip and rolled free. He came to his feet. Obayashi had also risen; he was again smiling, the same knowing smile.

They came together. Jan felt Obayashi's leg entwining about his own. He was exhausted and this time too slow. Obayashi threw him cleanly to one side, keeping Jan's leg locked momentarily in the air with his own. The full weight of Jan's body and the force of his fall twisted his leg at the knee—a knee that had already been surgically pinned and stapled.

Obayashi stood over him, motioning for him to rise. Jan came to his feet.

But the knee would not hold. Jan toppled back to the mat. He looked up. Obayashi was smiling. The room spun. And the comparison between Obayashi and Walter struck him again, just before he passed out.

It was three days since Bill's operation—three long days.

Dojna had walked with Bill to the door of the operating room. They had smiled as they parted: a mixture of worry and hope and the need for this operation to be a success.

Dojna thought about this as she walked down the hospital corridor to Bill's room. Today, Dr. Mead was to meet with them and assess the results of the surgery.

Dojna had stopped in the hospital chapel to pray—for strength to face this day, and the future. She hoped desperately that the strength she had prayed for would not be needed.

Dr. Mead was conducting his examination when she arrived in Bill's room. The bandages were off and he was gently touching the skin on Bill's stump with his fingers. Dojna viewed the one large scar that now covered the end of Bill's stump; the numerous little scars that had been there were gone. For a moment she looked with a professional eye. The surgery had been well performed, remarkably so. Then, she found herself watching with the eyes of a wife, anxious, worried—waiting.

Dr. Mead stopped his examination and made his short smile. "The surgery is fine," he said, "but the pain hasn't diminished, has it?"

"Maybe we haven't given it enough time," Bill said.

"The burning is still here?" Dr. Mead touched the end of Bill's stump.

Bill nodded.

"And the aching up here?" He cradled the stump in his hands.

Bill nodded again.

Dr. Mead took a deep breath and expelled it slowly. He shook his head. "We would have circulation by now. There would be at least a measure of relief if the surgery had succeeded. . . I'm sorrry."

Bill felt as if he was suddenly looking down from a very high place, about to fall—the same roller-coaster feelings he had experienced in the hospital just after the bombing. He fought for control.

"What now?" asked Dojna.

Dr. Mead shook his head.

Bill felt himself slipping and reached out in desperation: "If it were you, if it were your leg, what would you do?"

Dr. Mead took another deep breath and grimaced. He looked at Bill intently. "I guess I'd go to Mayo Clinic and try to get some first-rate diagnostic work done, try to get at the cause."

The words "Mayo Clinic" seemed somehow magic. Bill clung to them immediately, used them to stabilize the panic that had been building within him. He had no real knowledge of the clinic. But, just then, he needed something, anything, to keep his hope alive.

Dojna saw Bill's hope come to life, and she understood immediately. A part of her wanted to point out that the Mayo Clinic, for all its renown, did not practice magic; they offered no guarantee. But what else could Bill do but clutch at this hope. She had sensed the incredible depression that had almost engulfed him just a moment before. He had to hope with everything that was in him—it was self-preservation.

Dojna saw that Dr. Mead was having thoughts similar to her own. Their eyes met for a brief moment. Both remained silent.

Then, suddenly, Dojna found herself hoping and believing too, almost as fanatically as Bill. As a professional, she had great respect for the Mayo Clinic. And as Bill's wife she needed to hope and believe as badly as he.

She went and stood beside him. The Mayo Clinic—they would go.

9

Late 1971. Jan was drifting south. Georgia in November, then on to Daytona Beach in Florida as the northern winter he had left behind in Michigan began to touch the southern states. He was doing odd jobs, cooking for a few days, pumping gas—his savings had run out. He was still driving the Corvette, an expensive friend. The idea of selling it and hitchhiking had occurred. But there was no hurry, no hurry at all. He wasn't really headed anyplace in particular anyway; what difference could it make when he got there?

Tokyo and his quest for the Olympics seemed far behind, had never existed, really. He knew that now.

The injury to his knee had been severe. He had decided to return to the United States for treatment. Jan was well schooled in the workings of the knee. In his mind, he had a very good picture of what had happened.

A surgeon in Michigan confirmed Jan's diagnosis. The ligaments that connect the tibia, below the knee, with the femur in the lower thigh, and hold the knee joint in place, had been torn loose. His knee was free to swivel several degrees and could offer barely enough support for him to walk.

The surgeon asked the same question Jan had heard twice before: "What do you plan to do on this knee in the future?" If the answer was "compete," it meant surgery—the ligaments would have to be stapled in place to be able to withstand the rigors of judo. If the answer was "normal activity," the knee could be allowed to heal by itself. Jan chose the latter.

Even before he left Japan, he had known this would be his choice. The injury had forced him to become aware of his own feelings, feelings that had been just below the surface all the time. When he realized his injury would mean, at best, a long layoff and that he would not be fit in time for the Olympic tryouts, he was neither saddened nor dismayed. He was relieved. The feeling of relief was so strong it could not be ignored. And it forced Jan into further self-examination.

Judo had never been a legitimate pursuit. He had used it; first, when Walter was alive, as an escape, a place to hide from the life Walter had fashioned for him—and had fashioned him for. After Walter died, Jan had grabbed at it—the nearest thing—and had attempted to fill the incredible void Walter's death had left in his life. Jan had *used* judo. He had never loved it or been committed to it.

He understood this, now. It made him disgusted with himself. At a very deep level he had been disrespectful to the art of judo.

This was the same disrespect Jan had seen and despised in others since he was a boy: the lack of involvement and commitment at a very deep level in whatever one did. But now he understood more.

Discipline, alone, could not free one from the aimlessness he believed he saw in the people around him. Fanaticism would not substitute for commitment based on a genuine love.

Jan was unfaithful to the art of judo. He had brought to it fanatic discipline but no love or commitment. In his own mind he became no better than those he had always despised. And, as if for the ultimate punishment, he sentenced himself to wander.

The first impression of the Mayo Clinic was, for Dojna and Bill, as it is for most people, overwhelmingly positive; the highly structured organization of the clinic and town itself inspired confidence. And fueled their hopes.

The town of Rochester, Minnesota, is designed to serve Mayo Clinic. Facilities for handicapped persons are excellent: the airport, the taxi cabs, the very streets and sidewalks of the town. Bill and Dojna stayed at a hotel connected with the clinic by underground walkways. The schedule for his various examinations was waiting for Bill at the hotel desk when he and Dojna checked in.

First, Bill underwent a complete physical examination. The routine clinic procedures uncovered an adverse reaction Bill was having to the medicine he had been given during the mayoral campaign for his bloodshot eyes. It was a rare, but documented, reaction to a specific chemical in the medicine. Continued use would have resulted in severe glaucoma, possibly blindness. But the discovery had been made in time. There was no danger. Bill was simply to discontinue his use of the medicine.

Bill's regard for the clinic grew; also, ironically, did his general distrust of the medical profession.

Special appointments were scheduled for examination of Bill's stump. An orthopedic surgeon did the initial examination and quickly called in a neurosurgeon.

The neurosurgeon was a young man, very confident. He pressed his fingers into the end of Bill's stump, his head to one side in a listening attitude. For several minutes he continued this.

83

When he touched a certain place, Bill winced. The neurosurgeon pressed harder. Bill's entire body went taut.

The neurosurgeon stepped back.

"That," he said, "is a *neuroma*."

"A neuroma?" Bill asked.

"One of the nerves in your stump is attempting to regenerate," the neurosurgeon explained. "It has grown into a tiny ball and is causing you pain."

"Is this common?" Bill asked.

"Not uncommon," said the neurosurgeon; "regenerative powers vary from individual to individual. You have heard of persons losing the tip of their finger and having it grow back?"

Bill nodded.

"Your body is attempting this same feat with your leg. Here, of course, the magnitude of the task is far beyond the body's powers. The very tip of a finger or toe is the limit—and sometimes this does not happen. But the impulse is there. In your stump this impulse has succeeded in extending the length of a nerve. There is no place for it to go and it has formed itself into a ball."

"Can anything be done about it?"

"Fortunately, yes. It can be removed. A quite simple operation, actually. I'm sure you can find someone in your hometown to perform it."

"What about *here*?"

"The surgery could be performed in a local hospital. I could do it myself, if that is your preference."

"How soon?"

The neurosurgeon smiled. "I see you're a man who gets down to business. I've had a cancellation the day after tomorrow; would that be soon enough?"

The surgery was performed on November 15, 1971.

There was a large neuroma in the place the neurosurgeon had indicated. It was removed without complications.

But Bill was unsure about the success of the operation. His pain was, if anything, only slightly diminished. He and Dojna waited, hoping; afraid to believe it would get better, afraid not to.

Bill was released from the hospital three days after the operation. There had been no improvement. Still, they continued to hope. They waited. What else could they do? Bill listened with all his internal senses to his leg. At a given moment he would swear the pain was decreasing. But he could sustain this perception for only a short time, usually less than an hour; the pain was there, it would not be denied.

Bill and Dojna returned to Joliet. They arrived in the night. Tired from traveling and from the operation, and with the aid of a powerful sedative prescribed by the neurosurgeon, Bill slept more soundly than he had in over a year. But he woke screaming.

The pain in his leg was excruciating beyond anything he had yet experienced. He tore back the covers: the end of his stump had turned to a deep purple during the night; a sacklike protrusion, filled with liquid, grew from it—visibly pulsing. Bill's scream had brought Dojna fully awake. A glance and she knew: a *hematoma*, a blood clot forming outside the blood vessels. She packed Bill's stump in ice and called Mayo Clinic.

Three hours later they were on an airplane, on their way back to Mayo.

The hematoma was treated. In a matter of days the swelling was reduced. Several more days of whirlpool baths and wrapping and Bill's stump had returned to its normal condition—with all the pain, just as before. Nothing had changed. Bill informed the neurosurgeon.

The neurosurgeon, the man who had performed the operation and removed the neuroma, referred Bill back to the orthopedic surgeon, the original Mayo Clinic doctor Bill had seen. The othopedic surgeon called in a physiatrist, a doctor who specializes in physical medicine and rehabilitation and has a close connection to prosthetics.

"It's getting hard to tell the players around here without a scorecard," Bill said. But there was no humor in his voice and no one laughed.

Bill remained pointedly neutral while the physiatrist made his examination. The physiatrist examined, along with Bill's stump, his prosthesis and asked that Bill walk back and forth several times across the office.

Dojna sat in a chair, nearby.

"The problem is quite obvious," the physiatrist said.

Bill looked at him blankly.

The physiatrist went on, "The prosthesis does not fit, it is too long by a quite remarkable amount. I also think the knee mechanism is poorly adjusted. Perhaps there is more, but that will take closer examination."

Still, Bill said nothing.

"Mr. Barr," the physiatrist said, "is there something wrong?"

Dojna looked at Bill, caught his eyes with her own and held them. She bit at her lower lip and breathed very slowly.

"All right," Bill finally said. He turned to the physiatrist, "What do I do?"

The Mayo Clinic did not have a prosthetist on staff. Bill was sent with a prescription to a firm in Minneapolis.

Here, they checked his prosthesis for problems other than those discovered by the physiatrist.

The total-contact socket was found to be too small, and generally ill-fitted.

An entirely new leg was made.

By the time Bill finally received it, Christmas had come and gone. He and Dojna had stayed in Rochester, not really wanting to go home without the new leg. They talked to their children by telephone, but otherwise let the holiday go by unnoticed. It seemed somehow easier that way.

Bill had managed to regain a measure of hope, but only that. This latest doctor was the first to have examined the prosthesis itself. That made this time seem different. But, then, almost every doctor he had seen had a new approach of some sort. And that made it feel like all the others.

When he went to receive the new prosthesis, there was trouble fitting his stump into the total-contact socket. His stump had to be packed in ice before the leg would go on. It felt all wrong, and Bill said so. But he was assured everything was all right.

The pain not only failed to diminish, it became worse. Bill complained to the physiatrist.

The physiatrist assured Bill of the competence of the people who had built his new prosthesis, and referred him back to the orthopedic surgeon.

Bill was requested to come, alone, to the orthopedic surgeon's office—the same office he had come to originally, almost three months before. As he entered the office he noted, in the doctor, an air of stern resolution.

"We must assess the situation, you and I," said the doctor. "The hematoma was an unfortunate and painful complication but it does not alter the basic reality: there was a neuroma present in your stump; it has been removed. You should now have a significantly reduced level of pain. In addition, significant problems were discovered in your prosthesis—these have been corrected." The doctor drew himself up in his chair. "Let me be frank: I have watched you walk on your prosthesis—I do not believe you have ever accepted the prosthesis or the fact that it cannot ever replace your leg."

Bill's lips tightened, but he remained silent. The doctor continued.

"It is evident that you are a wealthy and powerful man. You are not used to not having your way. But you must face the fact that *no one* can restore your leg. No matter how many doctors you go to, no one can bring it back. Until you accept this I do not believe anyone can help you. You must learn to use your prosthesis and you must learn to live with some pain."

There was a purposeful silence on the part of the doctor. He waited for Bill to offer rebuttal. When Bill did not, he went on.

"I have scheduled you into our physical therapy department. They will make sure you know how to use your prosthesis correctly. The rest will be up to you. I have left instructions that you are to walk and walk and walk—until you have mastered this thing."

Bill nodded. His face burned and he fought back tears as he left the office.

"No," Dojna said, when Bill had told her the doctor's assessment and recommendation, "I don't believe this. He is wrong. This is not the answer."

"Maybe we're too close to it, Dojna. What if he's right? I've got to try."

Dojna was crying. She shook her head. But she understood, and she let Bill's decision stand.

Bill kept his appointment with the physical therapy

department. The facility was modern and clean. The physical therapists themselves were predominately young and wore bright-colored jackets.

Bill walked back and forth, back and forth, between the parallel bars, listening closely to the advice of the therapists. He climbed up and down the practice stairs that went nowhere. And he learned to sit and stand as if he were a new amputee. The therapists seemed cold and aloof, more taskmasters than teachers—perhaps because of what they had been told by the doctor.

On the second day of this intensive training, Bill's stump suddenly became very warm. There was a violent increase in pain. Against the instructions of his therapist, Bill left the training area and sat down and removed his prosthesis. It was filled with blood.

Bill had had enough. As soon as his stump had healed sufficiently to travel, he and Dojna left the Mayo Clinic.

They were going home. Neither of them made any mention of the future beyond that. They were out of energy and out of hope. They were numb. Neither one could even think about what they would do next.

On the plane, as they returned to Joliet, they did not even speak.

10

Dojna screamed.

Bill's body lay motionless on the bed. The bottle which had held the prescription of sleeping pills stood empty on the nightstand. It had been more than half full the day before.

Dojna gained control of herself quickly and ran to Bill's side. He was already deep in a coma. It was too late to induce vomiting. She reached for the telephone. . .

An hour later she sat in the waiting room of a private hospital. The events leading there were vague, somehow unreal within her mind. She recalled opening the apartment door for the emergency team; the flashing red and blue lights of the ambulance had followed them into the apartment. The siren; and kneeling beside Bill in the back of the ambulance—she remembered that. She had directed the ambulance to a hospital where a friend was the chief administrator and she knew many of the doctors. Bill was still a celebrity; Dojna remembered the mayoral campaign too well; she feared the press. Perhaps she could save him the ordeal of the press. . .if he lived. If. . .

And then he was being wheeled down the brightly lighted hospital corridor away from her, perhaps forever.

Dojna found the small meditation room in the hospital and prayed. She also remembered: from the first day she had met Bill forward, she remembered.

He had been so completely alive, so much in control—his presence the dominant factor in almost any group. He had always seemed physically even larger than he was. And after the bombing: the strength of his will had, for Dojna, only reinforced this picture. She could still see him standing on the bridge of their boat in the storm they had weathered.

But this picture was now alongside another: the final days of the mayoral campaign, Bill's eyes bloodshot and glazed, seeming to sink deeper and deeper into the dark hollows around them.

And then the doctors: Bill no longer marching but dragging himself from doctor to doctor, lying in one hospital bed after another, operation after operation, his body growing thin, his spirit being worn away. And now this.

Finally, Dojna went to the waiting room. She walked slowly, her face resigned.

She began to blame herself; she should have known. After the return from Mayo, Bill had ceased going to his office at all. He had been overusing the sedatives, staying, half drugged, in bed for fifteen and twenty hours a day. When he was up he only sat and stared, sinking deeper and deeper into hopelessness.

Dojna had seen all this. But she had been too exhausted, too depressed herself, to pull Bill up again with the strength of her will. Worried about the impending crisis in Bill's financial affairs, she had thrown herself into her practice, hoping to help here, at least. She had seen to Bill's basic needs, running home between patients to check on him—she had not known what else to do.

Now, looking back, she blamed herself completely. She should have been able to do something. Something, somehow. . .

Dojna sat in the waiting room alone. She had not called the children or Bill's brother and sister. Bill would not want them to be here. Perhaps they had the right. But Bill would not want it. She would not call them. She had made this decision; she would stick to it. Alone. And pay whatever consequences there would be.

It was three hours since Dojna had arrived at the hospital. The doctor came out, a colleague she knew well, a friend.

"We don't know," said the doctor. "We won't know for quite a while. If he'd just help us a little, if he'd just *want* to live, I'm sure he'd come around."

"He's been in constant pain for almost two years," said Dojna. "Would *you* want to live?"

The doctor looked down at the floor, uncomfortable, embarrassed.

"I'm sorry," Dojna said. "He *does* want to live, I know it. I'm sorry.

The doctor touched her arm. "Dojna, go home, get some rest, you're going to need your strength for later."

She nodded her head.

The phone was ringing when she arrived back at the apartment. She was sure it was not the hospital, not yet. She was exhausted and ignored it. It continued to ring. She stared at the phone, her mind trying to grasp something. It must have been ringing all night, she thought. Then suddenly, somehow, she knew. . .one of the children. Something had happened! She ran to the phone. . .

It was morning when Bill regained consciousness. He woke in a half world, suspended somehow between the living and the dead, not willing or able to deal with what had happened. He felt no relief at finding himself alive. Nor was he angered or saddened. He felt nothing at all. He remembered as a child being kicked very hard in the stomach by an older boy—he had laid on the ground long

92

after the boy had left, feeling very much as he did now: alone, deeply tired, but all other emotions locked safely away somewhere deep within him. Later, he had become fanatically angry and searched for the boy, a rock in his hand. But he could not remember what that felt like now—it was only a colorless picture in his mind.

He stared at the ceiling, ignoring the doctor and nurses around him. Time did not exist in the usual sense: no future, only a hazy sense of the present. Ironically, it was the pain in his leg that gave his mind its only hint of stability. The pain *was* there and it acted as a lifeline tying him, however weakly, to the real world.

Prodded by the pain, his mind wandered back through a nightmare version of the almost two years since the bombing. He could not sort out the distorted and imagined from the real, as if he were suffering from a very high fever.

The roller-coaster image that had haunted him in moments of desperation ever since the bombing returned: it appeared as an actual structure of concrete and steel with bright-colored passenger cars; he saw himself sitting atop the steepest grade but felt no fear. He no longer cared.

A seemingly endless progression of doctors walked through his mind, all talking at once. Bill found himself listening, trying to sort out their words, trying to find a missed clue to the source of his pain. He tried not to listen, tried to turn away, but he could not.

The memories of hospital beds and operating rooms and hallways filled with amputees being herded like cattle toward a man in a very white coat passed through Bill's mind. He saw himself back in the place where his first prosthesis had been made. And then all of the other places began to swim through his mind. The years of pain. . .and all at once he was burning with rage, a life-giving anger. Like a little boy with a rock, searching.

The room around him began to come back into focus. He acknowledged the doctor and nurses with his eyes. He remembered taking the sleeping pills, one by one, sitting on the edge of his bed. He acknowledged to himself what he had done. And he began to worry about Dojna, what had he done to Dojna?

Dojna. She was there in the room. Bill had slept, or passed out, and had regained consciousness again. His mind was clearer. Dojna could not hide what she had been through; on her face were written the waiting hours she had spent.

But her eyes were still soft; with her eyes and the slightest touch of Bill's cheek, she told him she understood: perhaps the greatest gift he had ever been given.

Then her eyes changed. A glaze of fatigue and tears came over them. Her face was suddenly filled with resolve, a reflection of the second impossible decision she had been forced to make in the last twenty-four hours.

"Bill. . .Bill, I have to tell you something. There's been an accident. Tony's been hurt—they've had to amputate his foot."

Bill reeled as if he had been physically struck; the room tipped and he felt dizzy and nauseated. Dojna's face became a blur. He fought for control, reached out his hand. Dojna took it. They held onto each other, fiercely.

Part Two

1972–

11

June 15, 1972, Del Ray, Florida. Tony Barr lay in a hospital bed. He lay very still, his face expressionless. The shades in the room around him were drawn, making it dark at midday. A week earlier his life, like a deck of cards, had been tossed into the air; the new order was too much too fast to absorb. . .

He had been standing, with a group of friends, on an old railway boarding platform; they had stepped out from a fashionable, converted depot restaurant to watch the train pass by. Tony stood near the edge. He remembered the roar and the groaning, metal screeching sounds of the train as it rounded a curve, nearing the old depot. He remembered the engine and several passenger cars, blurred almost together as the front part of the train passed him. Then something hard struck his arm.

And he was spinning, the right side of his body filled with a violent ache, the station and people becoming a blur around him. The noise of the train grew suddenly louder; and the ground struck him hard, a shock; it seemed almost to lift up and meet him. He was still moving, his body out of control. His left foot went under the train; and a wheel, in an instant of seering pain, cut his toes and a large part of his foot away. The spinning momentum of his fall continued and carried him back, inches clear of the track.

Several people dragged him back further. The back portion of his shoe remained strangely in place, still tied on what was left of his foot. His right arm was broken and a deep gash ran the length of his face. Something from the train had struck him. He did not then, and never would, know what.

Tony sat quietly staring at the ground. He was deeply in shock. He became vaguely aware that something was being wrapped tightly around his leg. There was no pain; he felt nothing. He continued to stare at the ground, never once looking at his foot. A very long time seemed to pass. He heard an ambulance off in the distance, and guessed that it was for him. Then he passed out.

When he awoke in the hospital, the surgery had already been performed. More cleaning than surgery, actually. The train had done most of the cutting. Yet Tony could still *feel* his entire foot, as if it were being smashed and cut, all over, again and again, as he lay there in bed. He felt if he threw back the sheet his foot, his entire foot, would lie mangled and bleeding before him. This image would not go away.

A doctor came in and told Tony about the amputation. Tony's heel and a small part of his arch had been saved—the rest was gone. But Tony could *feel* his foot so clearly. Within himself he refused to believe the doctor.

A nurse gave him a shot for the pain. He slept: a drugged, delirious sleep, waking for brief periods every few hours. Even awake, he was confused and disoriented.

He could not think or even see clearly. But he could feel his foot, *all* of it. And he clung to that.

On the morning of the second day, his head cleared. The pain was intense but bearable. He noticed the cast on his arm and felt the stitches in his face. The same doctor came and told him there would have to be another operation: more cleaning of cinders and other foreign matter imbedded deeply in his wound, as well as surgical revision of his amputation.

Again Tony was taken into surgery: this time seeing the white-coated doctors and nurses, only their eyes visable between mask and cap; this time feeling the anesthetist placing the rubber gas mask over his nose and mouth.

And again Tony awoke in delirium, reliving the accident.

Another day passed. Tony's head cleared and the pain returned, as before. The doctor talked of yet another surgical revision.

Tony asked the nurse to pull down the shades. He wanted to be completely alone, to isolate himself from even the daylight outside his window. He stared at the ceiling, not thinking, not feeling—protecting himself by withholding all caring, all hope.

It was like this that Bill and Dojna found him.

Jan walked from the room he was renting, through the penny-arcade streets of Daytona Beach to the ocean. He walked quickly down the main beach, passed a sign that forbade driving beyond. The sand became softer and the backdrop of giant motels changed to houses and trees. The surf was very white and very blue in the late afternoon sun, and Jan reminded himself not to hurry. He slowed to a thoughtful pace, watching the waves.

He had noticed about himself, of late, how intensely he did things. Everything! Even if he built a sandcastle, it had to be done efficiently—it had to be perfect.

He slowed his pace even more, becoming aware of himself and the sun and the afternoon breeze off the water. His knee had completely healed and it felt good to walk surely and strong.

"We make people walk," Walter had said. Jan heard him within his own mind saying it now. And felt for an instant the intense pride and sense of purpose he and Walter had shared. But he put it quickly aside. He was Jan Stokosa, not Walter—he would find his own way.

Walter, the healer and teacher; the tyrant—at least I understand now, thought Jan. No, he corrected himself, I don't understand at all; I just have it organized. . .

In late February, three months before, Jan had gone home to visit his mother. A letter had come for him while he was there from a long-time patient of his and Walter's, Bill Stieler.

Bill Stieler was an above-the-knee amputee, hit by a shell during World War II. Dissatisfied with his first two prostheses, he had, on the advice of a fellow amputee, sought out Walter. Jan had been a young boy helping his father when Stieler first came to be fitted. Walter succeeded where others had failed, and Stieler became his friend and enthusiast.

Stieler watched Jan grow into manhood, and, ultimately, when Walter retired into research, became Jan's patient. His letter read:

> Dear Jan,
> I know you are off traveling the world and only hope this letter reaches you in time. I have recently been to Colorado and have learned from a most re-

markable man, Hal O'Leary, to ski. That's right! Ski! This is managed by means of using one ski and a pair of "outriggers" (special poles with a ski tip attached at the base). I can't tell you what it has done for me to learn this. I have arranged for Mr. O'Leary to come to Boyne Mt. in Michigan to put on a clinic. I feel this has great potential for helping all amputees. Jan, I really feel you should be at this clinic. I only wish your dear father could be here for it too. Please be my guest for the three days of the clinic at Boyne Mt. You will find a room reserved in your name.

Your friend,
Bill Stieler

A mimeographed invitation was enclosed with the letter. Jan read his name, typed into the appropriate space: "Jan J. Stokosa, C.P."

He went to Boyne Mountain.

Jan stopped walking and realized it was getting dark. The breeze had a slight chill to it now and the startling bright colors of the ocean were beginning to fade. He sat down on the sand and stared out at the horizon: Bill Stieler had given Jan a new perspective, and he sensed that he must keep it.

Jan and Stieler had eaten dinner together on the final evening of the clinic. There had not yet been a great deal of time for talking. Hal O'Leary had kept them very busy.

The clinic opened each morning with a session conducted by O'Leary. The beginning amputee skiers were then paired with the more advanced participants, such as Stieler. Jan worked the rope tows and lifts, helping each amputee decide how best to handle them; the different amputations created different problems, but none that could not be overcome.

Jan also took instruction in "three-track," the name coined for amputee skiing. Already an advanced intermediate skier, Jan learned very quickly.

By the third day Jan was three-tracking the more advanced hills, and taking a hand in instructing beginners. Bill Stieler was everywhere, shouting encouragement and lending his hands. Everyone was in a mood of high excitement and expectation, most of all the amputee skiers themselves. It was the birth of something very important to many of these people.

Hal O'Leary was a person of great personal magnetism. He created and held with his own personality a center around which the exuberance of the clinic whirled. Jan considered him to be one of the greatest natural teachers he had ever known.

Bill Stieler and Jan took a final run together on the last day of the clinic and then met in the plush dining room of the lodge for dinner. Stieler's leathery face was still glowing from the cold, and the excitement. He was a short, strongly built man with sandy hair, still in his fifties. He was in excellent physical condition, and it showed in his movements. That he had only one leg seemed at once obvious and irrelevant.

Jan was excited too. His own natural intensity had found, for at least a few days, a focus. Something was alive in his eyes that had not been there when he arrived. It was what Bill Stieler had hoped to see.

They were drinking hot wine.

"Here's to three-track skiing in Michigan," said Stieler, raising his mug.

Jan raised his too, and they drank.

"And to Hal O'Leary," Stieler added, drinking again. "It's been a fantastic three days."

"He's an amazing teacher," Jan said.

"Remind you of somebody?" Stieler asked.

Jan thought for a moment; he could not answer.

"He reminds me, when he's teaching, of Walter Stokosa," said Stieler.

The surprise in Jan's face was evident.

"I suppose it looked different from your vantage," said Stieler, "but watching your father teach you when you were a boy—there's a lot of similarity."

Jan remembered how he had been introduced to Bill Stieler. He had been fifteen years old. Walter chose certain patients and requested that, after they had been satisfactorily fitted with a prosthesis by himself, they should allow Jan to build and fit them with a second. The limb was then given to the patient as a spare. It was within this arrangement that Jan and Stieler had met, and came to know each other.

"I remember," said Stieler, "how he used to stand there and watch you work, correct you, and tell you little things. Oh, he was rough in his criticism, where Hal O'Leary is gentle, but the total giving, nothing held back—that's where Hal and Walter are alike."

Jan saw it at once, almost as if Stieler's words had ripped a blindfold from his eyes. And suddenly a second comparison came bursting into his mind: the instructors at the Kodokan. No jealousy or guarding of knowledge, a complete giving—it was the same. This thought was barely complete when another began: Waseda University, Obayashi, the instructor who had injured his knee—the complete opposite. . .and yet Walter was like Obayashi too. That was what he had seen the day of his injury but had not been able to hold in his mind: Walter was *both*.

Jan was suddenly remembering the hundreds and hundreds of times Walter had told him about and then shown him and then allowed him to try some aspect of

fitting or constructing a prosthesis. Then the rigid fairness of Walter's response: if Jan succeeded, a new responsibility was his and with it the pride of his achievement. Walter had made sure that he understood both. And if he failed, he must begin all over and nothing was his, for nothing is what he had achieved. But the other Walter had been real too. . .

Memories, like dominoes falling, filled Jan's mind: the mad, brutal Walter killing Jan's dog, threatening Jan's life; and the strong and fair Walter, teaching him, giving him that which he treasured most.

"Jan," Stieler said, waving a hand in front of Jan's eyes, "where are you, boy?"

Jan blinked, almost startled, and then regained his composure. "I was thinking about my father," he said.

Stieler nodded.

They drank and talked, and Jan realized that Stieler had never known the mad, brutal Walter. He had known only the brilliant prosthetist, the good and fair teacher of whom he had spoken earlier.

"You know something, Jan," said Stieler, "Walter cried when I told him the leg you built was as good as the one he made. He tried to hide it, but there were tears in his eyes."

There were tears in Jan's eyes now.

Stieler was quiet a moment. Then he continued to speak. "I noticed something the last few days; I have to tell you, Jan."

Jan was silent.

"You belonged here," Stieler said.

It was totally dark now and still Jan sat by the ocean, watching the stars come one by one to the sky. He continued to think about his father—the two Walters tumbling about in his mind.

A part of Walter had selflessly given his knowledge and skill in prosthetics, perhaps even his devotion; Bill Stieler had shown this to Jan. And Jan, in his present state of aimlessness, was in a unique position to appreciate the worth of this gift.

But the other part of Walter was also alive in Jan's mind, threatening to take over his life and make him but an extension. Jan realized it was from this he had fled when Walter died. Walter's grip had not loosened, as he had always expected it would. Walter held him, even in death. And this struck fear.

Jan could feel the two Walters at war within him: one giving him freely that which he so badly needed, the other twisting and warping this gift beyond recognition, demanding Jan give up his self in blind loyalty and obedience to. . .what? Perfection? Prosthetics? Walter himself? Jan didn't know.

What he *did* know was the force within himself, pulling against this, pulling away—if nothing else he would be free.

It was late. The stars were out and filled the sky over the ocean. But morning was still a very long way off.

Tony would not look at them. He stared toward the shaded window.

"Son," Bill said, "son, look at me."

Slowly, Tony turned his face toward them. His blank expression began to give way. And then he was crying, first softly, and then with the full force of the emotions he had locked away. Bill walked to the side of his bed

103

and took his hand. Dojna opened the shades and then came to stand next to him also.

And Tony *knew*—in that instant he acknowledged it within himself: he had lost a part of his foot, forever.

12

Summer 1972. Jan ran on the beach each morning. All day he worked a construction job in the Florida sun. And in the evenings he lifted weights. He was pressing well over two hundred pounds, approaching the state of Michigan record he had once equaled while training for judo.

Physical conditioning had become the external focus of his life. He was once again in training. Again seeking excellence as an end in itself. But this time without self-delusion.

Jan recognized the familiar pattern: escape, not pursuit. He did not know what to pursue. He did not love, neither was he committed to anything. The constant physical activity made this easier to bear. That was all.

He thought of himself as a machine that had somehow become self-aware, but did not know its function—the machine preferred digging holes and filling them in to standing idle.

There were insight and a harsh honesty in this image. And perhaps the beginnings of self-respect.

Two hundred miles away, in Del Ray, Tony Barr was spending his summer in a hospital bed. Already, he had undergone four surgical revisions of his amputation. And now, from the waist down, he was in a body cast. Within the cast, Tony's left foot was twisted behind him and bonded to the back of his right calf—an attempt to graft skin over the wound where his foot had been severed. Even when the body cast came off he would not be able to leave his bed; his broken arm was healing slowly and remained in a cast of its own, precluding the use of crutches.

Tony's phantom pains continued, varying greatly from day to day in intensity. At times he still felt his foot being cut and torn, as he had right after the accident. More often he felt a cramping in his toes, as if they were all turned under and he could not straighten them back—he could *feel* his toes as clearly as ever in his life.

He had thrown back the sheet, many times, and stared at the toeless club of his foot. And still the pain and the sensation of his toes would persist: his internal sense of touch and his sense of sight were at war about the reality of his loss. But there was no longer any real question in Tony's mind.

The pains continued. But they no longer triggered the half-believing, half-hoping illusion that his foot was still whole. It was a fact now in Tony's mind: nearly six inches of his foot had been cut away. The pains served only to reinforce and remind him constantly of this reality.

Gratefully, Tony had many visitors. Both family and friends. They maintained in him, during the long summer months, a semblance of belonging to the outside world. There was comfort in the caring of so many people. But they could not stem the waves of depression that washed periodically over him.

From his window, on weekends, he watched brightly colored parachute canopies open and drift slowly down from the sky. There was a drop zone, only a few miles away. Tony watched and endured his isolation—and wondered about the future.

The surgeon had told him he would be able to return

to his former life, completely. "Some newspaper stuffed in the toes of your shoe and you'll be as good as new," the doctor had said. Tony wanted very badly to believe this, and at times he managed to. But more often he remembered the experience that had been his father's and was deeply anxious about how *he* would walk and what he would be able to do.

In another way, it was his father who had given him his strongest feelings of hope. Bill and he had had a long conversation on that day after the accident. Bill had taken a chair beside the bed. Tony could not really remember what had been said, but he could remember the hope and determination he had been given. Often now he reached from his own depression, back to that conversation. He clung to the feelings it had left in him.

Tony had never seen his father as intense as he had been on that day. Bill had spoken each word not to him but with him, as if Bill had needed the words too and had taken them back into himself—as well as given them.

Bill, his voice filled with emotion, had vowed to Tony that if there was a way on earth to be made whole he would find it, for both of them. Often, lying alone in his hospital bed, Tony thought of this.

Toward the end of summer, with his expectations set on going home, Tony was told he must spend at least another six weeks in the hospital: the skin graft had not taken and would have to be redone. And there was the possibility of yet another surgical revision.

Joliet. Bill had achieved an almost maniac level of activity, much like the mayoral campaign of 1970–71. Tony's accident had rekindled the spark that drove him; he was again at least recognizable as the dynamic business and political figure he had once been. But to those who knew him, it was clear that the physical agony he suffered was unchanged: his eyes were expressionless, a barrier, flat and hard, keeping the pain from his leg inside; the hollows around them were deep and darker than ever; and his skin was still waxen and pale. It was his energy and impatience, more than anything else, that resembled his former self.

Already, he had begun to reverse the trend of his business. Losses had been cut and slowly it was beginning to stabilize. Organizational changes were under way: through delegation, Bill was attempting to reduce dependency on himself—he was going to need time as well as money.

Bill was once again a man with a cause; in Tony, he had found a purpose outside himself. And it had grown.

Bill's experience of the last two years had crystallized, convincing him of the existence of a problem much larger than his own. He knew he had not yet begun to understand it. He could not even name it. But he *felt* it fully: he was an amputee; he had experienced a wide range of the facilities and care available, and he could not find adequate treatment—even with his means. What must the situation be for others?

The vow Bill had taken to help himself and Tony he had also taken, later, alone with his God, for other amputees. And this had further kindled his spirit.

He now had a focus outside himself, as well as within, and from this he drew strength and determination. It was an old pattern in Bill's life. He recognized the feelings. And welcomed them as alternative to the suicidal depression he had just come through.

Bill was starting again his search for mobility and freedom from pain. Already he had spent two years of his life and over $100,000. He understood the odds against him.

The difference, then and now, was in his approach. He was no longer rushing headlong. He no longer hoped wildly. The past two years had taught him the price of having his hopes too high too soon. He was now much more the tactician, planning what might prove to be a very long battle.

Bill began a list of doctors and prosthetists and a number of practitioners on the medical fringe—anyone he heard of or read about who promised even the slightest possibility of being able to help.

With Dojna's assistance, he constantly updated and prioritized this list, visiting each person and medical facility on it. He was methodically checking out leads, eliminating possibilities—searching for clues.

Somewhere there was someone who could help him. Bill clung to this belief, for he knew that without it he was lost.

The summer passed into fall. Jan continued to work as a laborer and ran each day on the beach. Weight lifting had dropped away to be replaced by bowling. Jan was introduced to the sport by some of the men he worked with. Several of them bowled regularly, and invited Jan one evening to join them. Soon he was fanatically involved in the game. Every night, for weeks, Jan bowled, building his scores quickly past the 200 mark.

Jan threw the ball with great physical force and concentration, creating within himself a moment of exquisite tension: the smooth sound of the ball on the alley, the very white, red-belted pins, waiting, so straight and perfectly arranged—then the explosion of pins and ball, loud, even in a building filled with noise. Jan felt with each ball the tension within him shattered, if only for a moment.

He was new to the game, and, for a short time, fascinated, almost addicted to the feelings it created inside him. But the newness soon wore away, and the intensity of his feelings lessened. Like weight lifting, bowling became only an occasional thing.

Jan became acquainted with a number of people in the Daytona area. He went to parties and on occasional dates. But his involvement with others was on the surface only. Inside, he remained alone.

One evening, feeling particularly restless, Jan visited a local *dojo* to practice judo. The old excitement came back in flashes throughout the evening: during a particularly well-executed throw or escaping a tough predicament on the mats. But the excitement died quickly; the lesson he learned in Japan reasserted itself within him.

Jan knelt in meditation with the others at the end of the session: the quiet look inward. He closed his eyes and tried to relax—and he knew immediately that he did not belong. He should not be there at all. Judo was too worthy a pursuit to be used this way, as a pastime. It was not *his* pursuit. *He should not be there.* He had already learned this. Jan wondered at how he could have come. Had his spirit gone blind? A super awareness of his own aimlessness filled him, an awareness of his *need* for direction and purpose—like a balloon within his chest that one day soon might burst.

Later that night, walking along the ocean, Jan thought about his father: an obvious thing he had never grasped came clear. He understood now why Walter had not maintained his interest in skating; why Walter had not fought harder to keep it a part of his life; why his father had not taught him to skate. As a boy, Jan had read in old magazines the accounts of Walter's skating triumphs, and had looked endlessly at the pictures—and wondered these things.

Now he understood. Skating, judo: the same.

Jan found himself with a new appreciation of Walter's involvement with prosthetics. He must have truly loved it, Jan thought, or he would have found an excuse to leave it behind, to move on. Jan thought about Walter's life and the internal forces that must have driven him. They were so much alike, he and his father—and so different.

The following week Jan found it harder and harder to keep his routine. The pointlessness of his constant activity became steadily harder to bear. His brief return to judo had triggered a new level of discontent. . .judo was *almost* what he needed, and that heightened his awareness of the need. . .it had spurred him to think more about his father. . .things were coming to a head. Since he had left Japan, and even before, it had been building.

Jan stopped going to his job. He stopped running on the beach each morning. He no longer shaved and he wore the same clothes for long periods of time. He felt at a crossroad. Lost. As if he would soon disappear within the emptiness inside himself: a panic he fought to keep under control.

One late evening he walked into a bowling alley. He checked out a ball and shoes, failing to acknowledge the attendant's hello. He began to bowl with no thought of keeping the score. Each ball he threw harder than the last, focusing his concentration. . .harder and harder, unable to shatter the tension within his chest. . .and then he was suddenly aware that the people around him were watching. The entire building had grown quiet, except for the crash of the pins and the ball on Jan's alley. He left.

Each day he felt *something* was going to happen. That

111

the pressure within him could not just continue to build. For the first time, he took out the funeral pictures of Walter. He spread them out on the bed in his room and spent long hours staring at them. Day after day he did this, letting the memories wash over him. Emotions: love and hate. It seemed endless.

But slowly it began to subside. There was no revelation, no insight—just a gathering calm, as the intense emotions and panic slipped gradually away. Each day the pressure in his chest seemed less. He did not know why. He shaved and began to dress neatly again. Food tasted incredibly good.

A demon had been somehow exorcised—Jan felt he would understand, later. It did not seem time to understand yet. The future was no longer frightening. That was enough, for now.

Jan walked a final evening on the beach and said goodbye to something—he wasn't sure what. He did not press himself to understand. He packed his suitcase, without hurry. Almost without thinking.

He drove north in the morning, vaguely headed for Michigan. But near Jacksonville, Florida, he passed a prosthetics shop. It was a small place, sandwiched in among apartments and stores on the outskirts of town. Jan drove around the block and parked nearby. He stared at the sign for a long time. And then went inside.

13

October 1972. After a total of eleven operations Tony was finally released from the hospital. And even then his arm was too weak to support him on crutches. He was confined to a wheelchair.

He moved to his mother's home in Fort Lauderdale, Florida. For three months his mother and sister took care of him. The combination of his foot and arm injuries made him almost a total invalid. Immobile and dependent on others for help with nearly everything, his bouts with depression continued. His own image of himself, so deeply entwined with his physical abilities, was doubly hard to maintain; the present cast dark shadows upon an uncertain future.

Tony had a recurrent dream about himself skydiving. At the beginning of the dream he was not an amputee. Joyfully he would dive from the plane and freefall, his memories creating a vivid image within his mind. Then he would pull the ripcord, feeling the cool steel of the D-ring and the tug of the opening chute. And then it all would change. Suddenly he was an amputee; he was afraid to come down on his stump. A panic would well up within him and often he screamed as he landed, waking himself. Always the same feeling remained, deep in his stomach, refusing to be put aside: *this had been his last jump.*

By Christmas Tony's arm had begun to gain strength. He was managing himself an hour or two each day on crutches. Then in the following weeks his strength and balance grew quickly. It was the new year, 1973—more than six months since his accident. And Tony was about to take his first step without crutches.

He sat alone on the bed in his room and stuffed newspaper into the toe of a comfortable shoe. He tried the shoe on several times, taking if off and adjusting the paper until it felt solid against his stump.

He stood. The balance was not hard to work out, a little back on the heel, and he felt fairly stable. It felt incredibly good to be standing. Then the first step: he came forward with his left leg, pushing off with his good right foot; his heel touched the floor, solid, well balanced. But the toe did not hold—there was no support when the front part of his shoe came down. He wobbled badly and fell to the left, catching himself on a dresser.

He tried again and the same thing happened. He reversed the process, leading off with his right leg. Midstep, when he had to shift his weight from his left heel forward, the wobble began, and this time he fell to his knees.

He got up and tried again and again, with no success. Within him a rage toward the doctor who had advised him to use the paper in his shoe was building. He tried to tell himself he just needed practice, but it was obvious the weight-bearing dynamics of a normal step were impossible. There was no way to control his foot with his heel off the ground.

Tony found that by using his left foot simply as a contact point, like a crutch or a cane, he could swing his right foot forward quickly and complete at least a rude approximation of a step. A slight hop brought his left foot forward again, and he could repeat the process. It was awkward and slow and caused considerable pain in his stump—but it was a walk, of sorts.

His feelings were terribly mixed. He was glad to be up

and walking at all. He was raging at the doctor for setting his hopes so high, and for knowing so little. . .and that frightened him too. The future seemed bleak; totally uncertain, at best. And on top of everything he felt deeply guilty for being discouraged and unhappy at all—his father had lost so much more.

Tony sat on the edge of his bed and stared down at his feet. The shoes made him look completely normal. Slowly, he took off his left shoe. The contrasting sight of his stump struck him abruptly, almost like seeing it for the first time. And suddenly all his emotions resolved into a single aching, childlike wish for it not to be so.

Tony consulted a second doctor, who sent him to the Davey Shoe Mold Company in Fort Lauderdale. A leather-covered, rubber-foam insert was built for his shoe, a $100 item which produced exactly the same effect as the newspaper. Tony continued his hop walk and made an appointment with a third doctor, a highly recommended surgeon in Boca Raton, Florida.

Tony had been selling real estate before his accident, and now resumed his fledgling career. He found it best to use crutches while meeting his clients. Without them, his awkward walk made people uneasy. On crutches he told people he had been in a motorcycle accident but would be "as good as new in a month or two." This seemed to put them at ease. He was learning quickly about being an amputee.

He found himself staying home a great deal. In public he vacillated between feeling awkward and angry. His awkward feelings led to embarrassment and apologies for being in the way. In contrast, his anger took the form of total disregard for others: people didn't understand or care anyway. Both responses made him feel badly about himself afterward. It seemed better to be alone.

Tony realized he had never really understood his father's situation. He had been right there with him, helping him, loving him. He had thought he understood. But now he knew better: the discomfort, the frustration, the sidelong looks from people around him. . .no whole person could really know. And Tony was deeply aware that his problem was only a fraction of Bill's.

He thought back to Bill, pushing ahead in those first days after the bombing. And he felt a new, deeper respect for his father's courage.

The appointment with the Boca Raton surgeon was in early March. After a series of X-rays and a long examination a second appointment, for consultation, was scheduled. Another week of waiting.

And now Tony was more anxious than ever. At first the hop walk had seemed a bearable inconvenience, until he could find a proper solution. But his stump had gradually become bruised and sore, and steadily more difficult to walk on. The wound had begun to seep fluid, then blood. The two socks Tony wore over his stump as a cushion had to be changed several times each day. The wound had to be constantly bathed and wrapped in gauze; a minor infection had already begun.

Tony returned to the doctor on March 17. He was shown into a large office with expensive furniture. His X-rays were clipped to a viewing screen on a credenza beside the doctor's desk. The doctor went directly to them. He was young and had a friendly manner.

"Tony, that's right, isn't it?"

Tony had taken a chair in front of the desk. He nodded.

"Tony, we've got a problem: you see," he said, pointing to the X-ray, "the angle of your stump is down."

Tony could see that his stump tilted slightly downward from the ankle.

"You're walking like this," the doctor continued, making his hand into a fist and bumping his knuckles against his desk, "instead of like this," he put his fist down on the desk so that his knuckles lay flat in a row against it. "This would be like a man with a complete foot walking on the ends of his toes—do you see?"

Tony nodded.

"Now, what we have to do, first of all, is get your stump flat on the ground. There is a surgical procedure we can try, a lengthening of the Achilles tendon, the cord that runs along the back of your heel. This might allow your stump to lift up the necessary amount."

"*Might?*" Tony said.

"I don't know for sure that we can gain enough," the doctor said. "But let's take this a step at a time."

Tony settled back to listen.

"I've talked to some prosthetics people. If we can get the stump flat they think you can be fitted with a prosthesis."

Tony started to speak but the doctor held up his hand.

"I know, that sounds very tentative, but it's all we've got right now. Let me give you the alternative."

Tony settled back again.

"To fit you with a conventional prosthesis, your foot would have to be taken off above the ankle—this is what normally would have been done in the first place."

For a moment Tony thought he was going to black out. A wave of nausea passed over him and he felt very faint. The doctor watched him very closely, until he was sure Tony had regained himself. Then he continued to speak.

"I'm sorry," he said, "but those are our options. I suggest we try the tendon operation, first."

117

There were too many questions spinning through Tony's mind. He could not grasp any one of them firmly enough to ask it. He just sat staring at the doctor.

"Why don't you take some time to think it over?" the doctor said.

Tony nodded and stuck out his hand, rather dumbly, he thought. He realized that along with the turmoil of other emotions that had been loosed within him, he had a strong liking for this doctor and a confidence in him. They shook hands, and Tony left.

The girl at the desk told Jan he could wait. Mr. Barnes was with a patient but would talk with him as soon as he was finished. Jan took a chair in the tiny waiting room. The furniture was old. The room itself was clean but badly in need of paint. There were no magazines. Jan had noticed there was no "C.P." after the man's name on the door and guessed the operator was not certified, a circumstance of which Walter had always vehemently disapproved. But not illegal, thought Jan. All the more chance he needs help.

Sitting outside in his car, staring at the sign, the word "Prosthetics" had nettled his mind, like a face that demands yet defies recognition. It seemed unfamiliar. Yet he knew it too well; it was almost as if the word was being reborn within him and growing again, with incredible speed, to maturity.

And then he understood. A crucial piece of the puzzle went into place; there were many still missing, but the outline was clear. The two Walters within him were no longer at war. Jan had chosen the one and purged the other. He could look at the word *prosthetics* and no longer feel the rod across his back, pressing him under this ban-

118

ner. The *need* to resist was gone. The Walter that remained only offered a gift: the commitment to excellence and prosthetics—either or both, perhaps neither. And that was the point. The push and pull that had condemned him to aimlessness were gone. He need neither mindlessly conform nor rebel, nor spend his life wandering. . .it was clear. He could *choose.* He was *free.*

With surprise, he suddenly knew that the night before he had said good-bye to a part of Walter. He had let the cruel, self-made deity he had been forced to worship as a child drift out over the ocean. . .and he had felt sadness. Love and hate were not so simple: he had loved this Walter too.

Jan had looked at the sign, "Prosthetics," and breathed very deeply. He could choose. He was free. All inclination to hurry was gone. He would get a job as a technician, not tell his employer he was already a prosthetist. If not here then somewhere else. Somewhere he had never been, somewhere he was not known. Prosthetics seemed a part of him; or, perhaps, it was he that was a part of it—perhaps neither. He would go slowly. Decide slowly. The world seemed so full of choices.

"Mr. Barnes will see you now." Jan was jarred from his thoughts. The girl was holding the door to an inner office open before him.

Tony and Bill and Dojna talked many hours on the telephone. Finally, Tony came to Chicago and the three of them consulted yet another surgeon. The verdict was virtually the same.

Tony's original doctor had saved as much of the body as possible, a common surgical bias. He had not understood the prosthetic implications. An above-ankle amputation would have given Tony an excellent chance of being fitted with a prosthesis and ultimately returning to normal activity. The below-ankle choice had left his stump at an impossible angle; balance was precarious and the ends of the metatarsal bones were being forced constantly down into the wound. Ironically, if it had been possible to save just two more inches of Tony's foot, the entire equation would have been changed. The angle would have been different, and a filler in Tony's shoe would have very likely produced an adequate walk. But this had not been the case; the train had taken too much of his foot.

The Chicago surgeon concurred that the operation to lengthen the heel cord and an attempt to be fitted with a special prosthesis was a plausible first step. But he cautioned that another amputation and a conventional below-knee prosthesis would be the only solution if this failed.

The decision was made. Tony would return to Florida and have the heel cord operation. He *wanted* to keep his ankle; medically sound or not, he found himself glad it had not been taken.

14

Dojna sat on the plane next to Bill. It was night and the first-class cabin lights were muted. A stewardess moved quietly up and down the aisle, talking occasionally in a low voice to one of the passengers.

A few hours before, Bill and Dojna had seen Tony off on his flight back to Florida. Shortly afterward, they had boarded another jet themselves. They were on their way to the medical center at Duke University.

Bill sat next to the window, staring out into the blackness. Dojna could feel his anxiety, almost read his thoughts: *Maybe this time. . .Tony. .Why? Always why?* She found herself thinking with him. *Maybe this time. . .*

They had been so many places, talked to so many doctors. Mostly they heard the same things over. Cortisone shots, more than anything else—the same treatment Bill had undergone at the close of the mayoral campaign in 1971. But they had tried again, anyway. This time from an orthopedic surgeon in Michigan—and again the shots had had no effect. Neuromas were diagnosed often. And there were frequent referrals to psychiatrists.

Bill had been to a hypnotist; he had tried acupuncture; massage; he had even had vitamins rubbed into the end of his stump. All had come to nothing.

He had, on his own, come up with a theory that the total-contact prosthesis he was wearing was the source of his pain. He deduced that the vacuum which held it in place was pulling and irritating the scar tissue in his stump. Bill sold this idea to an orthopedic surgeon and obtained a prescription for a *strap leg*—an older-style prosthesis held in place by a pelvic belt and straps.

Not only did his pain become worse, his mobility was reduced to near zero; and he found many public facilities, especially restrooms, almost impossible to use. The strap leg was soon stored in a closet, along with the rest of his growing prosthetic collection.

There had been more doctors, more prosthetists. . .but Dojna did not want to think of them now. Especially not now, en route to visit yet another doctor. Thinking about all the failures made it impossible to believe in the future. And she knew that she *must* believe. *They* must believe. She glanced at Bill—he still stared out the window—and somehow she knew that he was thinking about Tony. He was blaming himself. But it had seemed so logical to save as much of Tony's foot as possible, she wanted to say. They had all thought it was the correct course. . .and then she realized she blamed herself too; she prayed that Tony's upcoming operation was the right decision.

The "fasten seat belt" sign came on overhead. A single note sounded throughout the cabin, calling attention: they were coming into Cleveland, Ohio. Bill and Dojna were to change flights to go on to North Carolina and Duke University. Dojna's thoughts were turned back to the present.

They had only a half hour between flights, and they had to change airlines. The distance was too great for Bill to walk. Dojna dreaded, for Bill, the trip by wheelchair through the airport terminal: the assault on his pride. She felt it so clearly, more clearly perhaps than if it had been herself. She found herself wishing it could be her, just for a while so he could rest. . .and then the wheels of the jet were touching down.

Bill turned away from the window and looked at Dojna.

122

She smiled: almost a smile. He nodded and took her hand. *Maybe this time.*

The surgery to lengthen Tony's heel cord was scheduled for early June. Almost one year, to the day, from the time of his accident. He would be in a cast for six weeks after, and not until then would they know if the operation had been a success. The waiting ahead seemed interminable.

It was only a matter of weeks until the surgery. But Tony's sense of time was distorted: he was filled with so many fears. Each hour passed slowly. Nothing was of interest. He could not force himself to read or even to watch television. Tony felt his life almost standing still; and yet the operation, with a speed of its own, seemed to be coming steadily toward him. He found himself, one moment, wanting the time to go more quickly; and, then in the next, wishing it would stop altogether.

He worried that his phantom pains would return; it was so gradual that they had subsided, and only recently that he had had long periods without them. He dreaded the operation itself, especially the anesthesia: the long, nauseating, half-waking return from the dead. And the pain. Eleven operations the summer before were still fresh in his memory. He remembered them all too well; they had left in him feelings not easily dispelled.

But even more deeply, Tony feared the operation would not succeed, that there would be months of uncertainty; and that, after all, he would be told his entire foot must be taken. At times he felt the doctors already knew this was where it would end; that the heel-cord lengthening was only a ritual to ease him toward another amputation. At these times Tony wanted the uncertainty to end. Let them take his foot off and be done with it. But then abruptly his feelings would change; and he would desperately want to keep what remained of his foot. Sometimes he felt he would not let them take it—even if he never walked.

Tony withdrew more and more into himself, confused and frightened by his own feelings. His foot was ulcerated badly, oozing fluid and blood; the hop walk was causing him increasing pain, and he feared he would have to go back on crutches altogether for the remaining days before his operation.

Tony's spirit was nearly exhausted. His months in the hospital and the initial failure of his rehabilitation weighed heavily; the fresh onslaught of fear and worsened pain—the waiting for yet another operation—was increasing his burden. Panic set in. He woke in the night, just three days before the operation, and found it difficult to breathe. A band seemed to be tightening across his chest. His mouth was dry. The ordeal before him seemed too much.

He rose from his bed and made his way out to the porch. He wanted fresh air, but the Floirda night was hot and offered none.

He needed something to hang onto; anything! He looked within himself. But his doubts and fears had already dissolved any small optimism or hope he had ever possessed. He felt empty and weak. He wanted someone to turn to. But there was no one. Others, he felt, would not understand. How could they? And he *would not* call his father. Bill's situation was so much worse than his. How had his father held on for so long?

Tony began to undertstand how alone Bill must have felt; must still feel. He thought of the time just after the bombing; he and Dojna and Robin had been able to support Bill, but that was all. The initiative had always been Bill's—it had to be, Tony realized this.

He remembered Bill in a wheelchair right after the bombing, announcing his candidacy for mayor to a roomful of reporters. For a brief moment, Tony could touch, almost hold, his father's courage—and he understood it.

Tony looked again within himself. *No one* else could face this for him. He must find the strength to face the future inside himself.

An idea came into his mind. At first, it seemed totally mad; then gradually this feeling faded, for the idea, in an odd way, made perfect sense. Tony knew that his father, at least, would understand, regardless of what happened. He remembered Bill's words from a conversation they had had in the past: "This skydiving, it's not just a hobby, it's important to you, isn't it?"

In his mind, Tony had already begun to pack his chute.

Tony drove to the little drop zone, just outside Del Ray: the same drop zone he had watched parachutes drifting above from his hospital window the summer before. His decision to jump was already made. He did not question it as he drove.

It was a Saturday afternoon. Tony knew there would be a large number of people at the drop zone. He stopped his car near a deserted hangar and changed into his jump boots. Then he drove on down the edge of a grass runway to a small, open-sided hut. The hut was surrounded by perhaps a dozen cars and about thirty people. A small plane was taking off as he pulled up.

The familiar sound of the plane gaining altitude seemed almost a greeting. Just the feeling of being there was intoxicating. Tony hauled his gear out of the back seat of his car and, using his hop walk, began to get ready. He

125

trailed his shoot out to full length and shook out the panels; and then began carefully to pack it, hauling it in and adjusting the large rubber bands that kept it in order within the chute.

Overhead, the steady drone of the plane's engine changed pitch. The pilot was throttling back, slowing for the jumper's exit. Tony automatically looked up.

Three black dots, all at once, and then a fourth, appeared in the air below the plane. Tony found himself counting: one thousand, two thousand, three thousand, four thousand. . .the dots were getting nearer to each other; slowly the first two came together, then the third dot joined them, the fourth was still hanging above. . .fifteen thousand, sixteen thousand, seventeen thousand. . .the fourth dot was closing the distance, and then all four were together. They were much lower now and Tony could see the linked arms, forming a star. The jumpers fell in formation for several seconds, their bodies growing ever more distinct—and then they were tumbling away from each other in backward rolls through the air.

The chutes began to open; first one; then two more, almost at once; and finally the fourth. Reds and greens and blues filled the air, growing steadily brighter as the jumpers drifted down toward the hut and the little knot of people and cars.

Tony realized how very good he felt. The panic of a few hours before had left him. He wanted, *needed*, to make this jump. He was confident he would have no trouble in the air. And he refused to think about landing. He was going to make this jump, and he would pay whatever it cost to come down.

The group of people near the hut had also been watching the sky. They now turned, as the jumpers floated above them toward a circle of soft sand beyond where

Tony was standing. Several people ran to help handle the chutes, and a number of people noticed and recognized Tony. Soon he was standing in a small group of friends, being welcomed.

Another star was going up, and Tony was asked to be one of the four. Fourth man, in fact: the position usually taken by the best jumper—a compliment. No one mentioned his accident or asked about his foot; his friends seemed to sense that he wanted it that way.

The jumpmaster, also a friend of Tony's, eyed him suspiciously as he hop walked out to the plane with the others.

"You sure you're okay to go up?" the jumpmaster asked.

Tony nodded. "I'm sure," he said.

The jumpmaster said nothing, but held Tony with his stare. An uncomfortable moment passed.

"It's okay," Tony added, trying to smile.

The jumpmaster scowled and continued to look suspicious. But finally he nodded and stepped back, allowing Tony to board the plane.

The climb to above seventy-two hundred feet took several minutes. Tony looked at the faces of the other jumpers, two men and a young woman. All friends from before the accident. They smiled back at him. A certain level of anxiety, mostly excitement, filled the plane. But there was nothing in the other jumpers that indicated any special concern. They were giving Tony this jump, like any other. Tony settled back and listened to the noise of the engine, feeling, all at one time, happy and excited and strangely content. He had pushed any worry about how he was going to land far back in his mind.

The plane leveled out and the three other jumpers began to move carefully into position. They crouched beside the doorless opening in the side of the plane, studying the ground. A minute passed, then two; one of the jumpers signaled the pilot with his hand. The plane slowed.

One by one, they eased out the door, hanging by their hands from the plane. Tony moved up; he scanned the three faces behind their goggles. They were ready.

Tony gave the signal and all three dropped away from the plane; he dove head first after them.

In freefall there is not a great feeling of speed, although the terminal velocity of 120 miles per hour is reached almost instantly. It is quiet and free. Tony maintained a head down, diving position, maintaining maximum speed to catch the others. He watched the three jumpers below him drifting together, their bodies arched to slow their air speed; in the back of his mind he was automatically counting...four thousand, five thousand, six thousand...they had thirty seconds before they must open their chutes.

Tony was super aware, as always in freefall: adrenalin-rich blood heightened every sense, revealing details and creating impressions unknown to the earthbound. The jumpsuit colors below him seemed totally new, as if a black and white picture had suddenly burst into brilliant yellows and blues, reds, and incredible whites; the earth, farther below, was a vaguely green blur. He could feel his heart beating, and his fingertips tingled against the rush of the air. He could *feel* his body, so alive, yet precisely under control. He felt confidence: an almost physical presence within him.

He found and touched and held an image of himself: able and strong. He caught a fleeting glimpse of something inside—*that he was.* Such feelings had been blurred with the loss of his foot, then lost entirely, until now.

The three bodies below him had come together, each holding the wrist of another. Tony arched his back and spread out his arms and legs, slowing his body perceptibly. He was still facing down but no longer diving. The others, their bodies creating between them a circle three-quarters closed, were directly beside and below.

Tony gradually pulled in his hands, slightly increasing his speed, and dropped into the star. . .twenty-one thousand, twenty-two thousand, twenty-three thousand. . .they fell, joined together, smiling broadly at each other and their accomplishment.

And then they were tumbling backward in four directions, gaining distance away from each other. The bright-colored chutes, one by one, popped open and drifted lazily down toward the little hut and the circle of sand behind it.

Tony handled his chute expertly, almost without thinking, directing it down toward the sand target. He watched the orange groves, passing below: green balls all laid out in rows as seen from the air. Beautiful. He breathed deeply.

Not until he was directly over the drop zone did Tony allow himself to think about his foot. He winced involuntarily as he imagined his stump making contact with the ground; but he did not panic.

The landing was painful. Tony managed to absorb most of the shock with his right foot and leg. But his left foot still touched down with considerable force; the end of his stump was torn open—no worse, perhaps, than if he had walked on it steadily for a long time. Blood oozed, warm, into his shoe; and it hurt. It hurt a great deal. Tony pushed back the pain, ignoring it as best he could. He stayed on his feet and returned the smiles of his friends, touching down around him.

15

Jan went to work as a technician, three days a week in the small prosthetics shop near Jacksonville. The owner of the shop had hired him on a trial basis, then quickly offered him more work. But Jan refused. Three days a week seemed enough: for the first time since he could remember, he was not in a hurry.

The work was comparatively simple. Barnes, the owner, took the plaster cast of the amputee's stump. He mailed this, with an approximate length, to a company in California. There a central lab converted the cast into a plastic socket, and—in the case of an above-knee amputation—attached it to a length of pipe and an artificial foot; the pipe was sectioned into two parts with a device for adjusting length and pitch, set in place of a knee. Below-knee and arm amputations were handled in a similar way.

When this temporary limb came back by mail, Barnes met with the amputee and made the final length and pitch adjustments. Jan then finished the limb in the basement workshop. He fashioned the permanent components from wooden blocks on a band saw; he affixed the necessary hardware, and coated the finished limb with plastic.

Jan enjoyed the familiar work. The tools seemed old friends, almost coming to life in his hands. He took great satisfaction in the skill with which he performed each individual task; the work itself felt very good. But he was highly dissatisfied with the final product.

The assembly-line sockets haunted him constantly. He

knew that the original castings Barnes had taken had not even been "marked," a procedure for locating and allowing for special characteristics of an individual's stump: exceptional muscular development, prominent bone structure, and unusual soreness. The comfort of these sockets would be inferior; it was possible that they might even *create* unnecessary pain. This was wrong. Jan felt, as he knew his father would have: this was not a matter of interpretation; there was no room here for differences. *This was wrong.*

Also, outmoded technology was being used almost exclusively: straps and hinges. Patients were not even being made aware of such things as total-contact sockets and hydraulic knees, or any number of other innovations; Jan wondered if Barnes knew about these things himself.

Worst of all, Jan knew from watching the patients walk that their limbs were not being aligned properly; and that this could create a variety of long-range medical problems in the back, as well as in the stump itself.

This was a side of prosthetics Jan had never seen, another world from the way Walter and he had practiced. He was repelled by it, yet, at the same time, strangely compelled to experience it. Jan kept his own counsel; he simply did his work and listened and watched, at first.

He confirmed his guess that Barnes was not a certified prosthetist. Barnes had learned prosthetics as a helper in another office, and had then gone off on his own. Jan could almost hear Walter voicing a constant complaint, but only when the two of them were alone: "You have to have a license in this country to clean teeth and fit eyeglasses: you even have to have a license to catch fish—but *anybody* can hang out a sign and practice prosthetics!" Jan had listened to Walter say this so many times but he had never really heard him, until now.

Jan worked and watched for several weeks before making his first suggestion. He felt he had learned the operation and had numerous ideas for upgrading it. He had also learned something from Barnes in these weeks, and decided to start with a very small suggestion.

Barnes' procedure was to have Jan shape the calf or thigh components of a prosthesis to a few standard sizes and shapes, according to the age and sex of the patient. In some cases this proved adequate, and a fairly close match to the remaining leg was provided. But in many cases—individuals overweight or otherwise of unusual size—the match up was atrocious. Jan showed Barnes the procedure for making a perforated tracing of the patient's good leg; by simply turning this over, a corresponding picture of the missing leg was produced. The prosthesis could then be constructed more exactly to fit the individual.

Barnes did not like the idea. The total time for constructing the prosthesis would be increased. That meant more cost, less profit. Barnes reminded Jan that he was a businessman; and that he had been building limbs successfully "long before Jan Stokosa ever came along."

Jan swallowed his angry feelings—at least for the moment—and went back to work. He would not leave. He felt he must stay awhile longer, although he could not exactly put his finger on why: something more there to learn, perhaps; something about this place he must understand more completely.

Jan stayed on at the Jacksonville prosthetics shop for several weeks more. He introduced a number of new procedures in the workshop and changed several of those that were already established. Barnes noted this silently, not approving but allowing the new practices to continue. Barnes was more than pleased with the quality and

132

amount of work Jan was producing. And Jan had his own reason for staying. The relationship between them was strained but not broken.

Jan continued to make polite suggestions, without success. Each time, the ill feeling between him and Barnes grew worse, and was followed by a period of mutual silence. Jan questioned the wisdom of staying on, yet he felt that this experience was teaching him something, something he could not yet name. The tension continued to grow—and then finally, over a problem patient, the inevitable break came.

A young Vietnam veteran—below-knee amputation—was having great difficulty using his prosthesis. He could remain on his feet for only a short period of time and was in constant pain. Although he was otherwise physically strong, three hours was the maximum he could stand or walk at any one time. Jan recognized him as one of the unexplained twenty or so percent of all amputees: the problem cases. Jan had worked with many such cases; the Stokosa practice, both under his father and then by himself, had had a wide reputation for dealing successfully with problems.

Barnes had made a series of unsuccessful attempts to correct the young veteran's prosthesis. He had repositioned the straps that held the prosthesis in place, moving them slightly higher above the knee; and then he had added more straps, connected to a pelvic belt. In the stump socket itself, he was using "moleskin"—a supple, leatherlike cloth—to pad and shim the gaps and create a better fit.

Jan had done the strap modifications, at Barnes' direction. He had noticed the moleskin in the socket, and, having happened to see this particular patient walk on several occasions, he had pieced the problem together in his mind. Barnes did not confide the details of any case to Jan, and the basement workshop kept Jan largely isolated from the patients. But this case was of special interest, the constant modifications made it so. Jan learned the patient's name from a work order and read his file—a practice he had been neither invited nor forbidden to do.

The discussion opened one afternoon in the workshop: "How's Jerry Turner coming?" Jan asked. The question itself struck a chilling note between them. Barnes stiffened noticeably. There was an air that this was none of Jan's business, almost as if Jan had been spying.

"He's coming fine," Barnes said. "Why do you ask?"

Jan had seen Turner leave from his last appointment. He had not been fine at all. Jan put down his tools. Feelings he had not expected were gathering inside him. He realized, quite suddenly, that because of Barnes' position he had been unconsciously maintaining toward him a tone of respect—and that the man did not deserve it. For the first time he spoke directly.

"I ask because Turner walks poorly. He is obviously in pain. And we keep cobbling up his prosthesis."

Barnes' anger was instantaneous. Jan's words triggered all the ill feeling, accumulated over the weeks. Barnes suddenly felt the full weight of Jan's suggestions and constant changes in procedure. Jan's manner had been polite. But what his words and actions had implied, right from the beginning, was not. Barnes' face was red.

"Just who in the hell do you think you are, coming in here and telling me how to run my business?" he said.

A part of these words struck home. Jan knew that he was sailing under false colors; he had never revealed that he was a prosthetist himself. But this didn't change the issue at hand.

"It's not a business," Jan said. "It's a *profession*. And you seem to know precious little about it."

"And you do?" Barnes asked.

"I do." Jan said.

"And just what would you do differently for Jerry Turner?" Barnes asked. "What would you do, Mr. *Technician?*"

Again Jan was struck in the face with the fact that he had misrepresented himself. About that, he was in the wrong. But *only* about that. Barnes' question had been obviously facetious. Jan gave it a serious answer.

"First of all," he said, "I'd do a decent casting. I'd build the socket myself and it would *fit*. I'd use an elastic sleeve to hold the prosthesis in place and get rid of those ridiculous straps. Then I'd align the damn thing so he could walk on it!"

Barnes was stunned for a moment, trying to digest the barrage he had just absorbed. As he gathered himself to speak, Jan sensed what was coming.

"Don't bother," Jan said, "I quit!"

The drive back to Michigan was time to reflect. It was the spring of 1973; nearly two years since Jan had left for Japan and the Olympics. It seemed like a lifetime ago. Even Florida—Daytona Beach and Jacksonville—seemed already to be clearly a part of the past.

He had stayed in Jacksonville longer than he had intended. The time had passed neither quickly nor slowly; it was almost as if the time there had not existed; a necessary waiting until certain things within himself became clear: his future direction. He had already spent enough time with the past.

Jan drove slowly. He stopped frequently to breathe in the springtime and look at the scenery; the mountains of

Kentucky held him for almost a day. He had come, in two years, a very long way. But now there was a lifetime ahead. And much more that he must understand.

Jan's stay in Jacksonville had left him with mixed feelings—about a great many things; and new ideas.

Jan had never worked with anyone but his father, and he was beginning to realize how sheltered a professional life he had led. He had seen poorly made and badly fitted limbs before, many of them—a great percentage of the Stokosa practice had been problem cases, and the patients often brought their previously made limbs with them—but Jan had never thought past correcting the immediate problem, until now.

Now he marveled at how he had been able to remain so blind for so long. He had seen the larger problem with his own eyes, touched it with his own hands as he worked; and he had been *told*: case histories, story after story of widespread incompetence and lack of concern—his patients had told him. He had listened, but he hadn't heard.

Incredibly, it was Walter who had taught him to turn a deaf ear, taught him the *professional* deafness of one prosthetist hearing about another—Jan sensed a deep and troubling contradiction here. Walter, whose dedication to prosthetics had been infinite, had taught him to look the other way. Jan stared in amazement at this realization.

In private, Walter had scorned the previous care of many of his patients and had spoken passionately about the generally poor state of the art of prosthetics; in private he had spoken this way. But in public never. Walter had even used the poorly made limbs brought in by patients as a part of Jan's training. Walter had used them to demonstrate to Jan the necessity for his own time-consuming and expensive techniques.

Walter had often spoken vehemently to Jan about the inadequacies of prosthetic training and certification. But, again, never in public.

And Jan had been trained to behave the same way in public. Even when asked directly by a patient if past care had not been deficient, one said nothing. The rules had been strict, and Jan had been taught them at an early age. More than taught, they had been handed down as an inseparable part of the religion of prosthetics: a canon of professionalism. Jan had virtually absorbed it, without question. Psychologically, an area of his perception had been muted. The stories told by his patients had had no impact, until now.

Jan felt the contradiction deeply. He did not understand. He could not reconcile his father's teaching and the reality of his recent experience. Barnes had ignited a fire that, ironically, Walter himself had laid. It was the commitment to excellence and concern for patients that Walter had passed on, the knowledge and skill and experience that Walter had imparted; and Walter's words, in private, about the profession of prosthetics—all this had prepared Jan to burn with anger at what he saw in Jacksonville. And yet it was also Walter's teaching that restrained him.

Jan had had the impulse to call Jerry Turner, and a number of Barnes' other patients, and advise them to seek help elsewhere. But something had held him back —something he was just now beginning to understand, and question. Jan sensed that he would always regret that he had not interfered in Jerry Turner's case.

Jan did not believe that Barnes was an evil man. Barnes had seemed decent enough in most ways. Even in prosthetics he was doing what he thought was a decent job.

But it wasn't a decent job, and his patients were suffering for it; and *that* was evil.

And the problem went far beyond Barnes. Barnes had simply provided a face for what Jan had unconsciously known. Barnes had made the broader world of prosthetics alive and real. Jan had lived, until now, on a professional island.

Jan thought about his father's early career, working for others: the internal price a man like Walter must have paid to be subservient; to have had to tolerate interference with his pursuit of perfection. Walter's career Jan now understood—the constant changing of employers, why Walter had ultimately formed his own practice. Perhaps that was part of why Walter would not speak out about prosthetics. Perhaps he was ensuring his isolation, guarding his hard-won professional autonomy. Jan began to understand and appreciate, more deeply than ever before, the gifts of knowledge and pride—and the freedom to use them—that he himself had been given.

Jan thought about his own unique, and uniquely expensive, apprenticeship: building duplicate limbs to be given away. He thought of the months he himself had worn a specially constructed prosthesis, so he would understand from the patient's viewpoint. And he felt the irony of not having been able truly to hear his patients when they talked to him of recurrent difficulties they had encountered with prosthetic services in the past. He had been able to see the situation of each individual amputee so clearly, and yet he had not been able to see the situation of amputees in general at all; nor been willing to face it, he thought.

Why had his father trained him this way? The question, unanswered, still nettled Jan. There were so many answers: fear; blind conformity. Had Walter been selfish?

138

Perhaps it was only *his* patients that Walter was capable of caring about; perhaps he was only caring about himself through them. But then why, in private, had Walter expressed such concern about the state of prosthetics in general. Jan was certain that this had not been just anger at those for whom Walter once had to work. Nor had it been mere elevation of himself over others. Walter's concern had been genuine.

Then why? Jan could not answer. He sensed that there was truth in all of the answers, and he realized that his understanding of his father had only begun. Even with Walter's madness put aside, banished, admittedly not understandable, the Walter that remained was complex; multifacets of dark and light hue. Jan remembered his own sadness at letting the mad Walter go that last night on the beach in Daytona—and Jan faced something within himself: perfection, like absolute evil, does not exist. Even the good and fair Walter that Jan had separated out and elected to keep within himself had been but a man.

With great satisfaction Jan realized he was thinking for himself: he was neither rebelling against nor blindly conforming to his father. He could feel Walter's influence strongly, but it was the influence of a man—neither god nor devil. Much of what Jan was feeling he and Walter shared in common. But there were also important paths of divergence. And Jan felt a keen sense of responsibility to resolve them.

What is a prosthetist? he asked himself. Does the fact that someone sells artificial limbs make him a part of my profession? *My profession.* Jan realized, for the first time, that he had made the decision about his future. And it felt very right.

Profession, not business, he thought. And it struck him that Walter had remained relatively poor all his life. Jan thought of Barnes pulling up to the little shop in Jacksonville in his Cadillac. Barnes was affluent. How incredible, Jan thought, realizing that he had never even noticed: Walter hadn't taught him a thing about business. "Profit margin"—Barnes had used the term often—was an alien concept.

Business: the very word seemed to throw light on the problem with which Jan had been grappling. In his mind, he compared Barnes' operation to his father's. Jan's pay in Jacksonville was low, slightly less than usual for prosthetic technicians; his wages as a laborer in Daytona Beach had been higher. Tools and working space had been at a minimum. The entire shop was geared to produce a high volume of low-cost limbs.

Walter, on the other hand, had constructed each prosthesis as an end in itself. Each prosthesis had to be the very best he could make it; and *that* had governed all. Walter had charged the going rates, sometimes even a little bit more, and much of the time he had still lost money. But where was the alternative?

Jan was dealing with the difficult questions of truly having a profession. He had never done this before. Walter had always resolved these questions for both of them. But no more! It had taken nearly two years for Jan to find his way back; back, but not to an island. He felt the need and the responsibility to involve himself in the larger world of prosthetics, to face the problems of his profession, perhaps even to break new ground; he had found his way back—*his* way back. And he was *free*.

The larger world of prosthetics fascinated Jan; he found himself thinking about the amputee ski clinic he had attended with Bill Stieler and it took on new meaning. He found himself suddenly very excited. It was at once wonderful and serious and frightening. He felt as if it were the beginning of his career: looking forward to his very first patient. And yet he could feel within himself the strength of his experience and Walter's teaching, and that created more the feeling of return. He sensed that both feelings were true; it was neither the beginning nor the end of his odyssey.

Jan was driving faster now. There was so much to think about, so much to do, so many problems to be solved. What could one person do? *All that he can*, a voice from somewhere within him was saying. The voice, of course, was Walter's.

16

Tony went into the hospital on June 8. The next day he underwent surgery. His heel cord, the Achilles tendon, was notched, twice on one side, once on the other, and stretched. The angle of his stump was elevated and frozen in place with a plaster cast that ran almost to his knee; the cast would maintain the new angle until the heel cord and surrounding muscles had time to adjust. The surgeon of record was the Boca Raton doctor who had first recommended this operation.

Tony woke from the operation with the cast in place. His first feeling was relief: the phantom pains had not returned. He had gone under the anesthesia, fearing, almost more than the operation itself, that the pains might be there when he woke. His first thoughts were of the eight weeks that lay immediately ahead; it would be August before the cast came off, and only then would he know if the operation had been a success. He was not glad for the wait. But he was already resigned to it.

He felt within himself a cautious optimism. The recent parachute jump was still fresh in his mind, making him feel alive; it stood as a symbol that he was still capable of participating fully in life; and it served as a punctuation mark, setting apart that first disastrous year after his accident and putting it behind him. He was looking ahead with hope.

The day after the operation Tony left the hospital. On crutches, he resumed his life. He returned to his job. He spent time with friends. He even managed to ask one of the nurses from the hospital for a date, his first since the accident. She accepted.

Tony had vowed to himself that he would not just sit and wait. He had almost committed that particular kind of psychological suicide before waiting for this operation. He was determined not to repeat the experience. Within himself he walled off all negative possibilities for the future. He focused on the idea that the operation would prove successful, that he would be well fitted with a prosthesis, and that he would return to a normal life.

This was going to work. It had to.

The time passed, if not well, at least tolerably. Tony maintained his positive outlook, almost to the end; and he did not isolate himself. The impulse to withdraw from others was there, but he did not give in. He kept close contact with his family and friends. He kept busy. Only during the last few days did he feel the need to use the mild sedative he had been given to help him sleep. The nights, so close to the time when he would *find out*, brought on attacks of anxiety. During the day he regained control, and even a portion of his optimism.

On August 3 Tony returned to the hospital. A medical technician cut his cast away with an electric saw: the bright steel circular blade cut neatly into the cast; it droned, and made a high-pitched whirring noise as it bit into the plaster. Tony watched with a peculiar intensity. He was thinking about the saw the doctor would use if, in the end, what remained of his foot had to be amputated. . .the wall he had built against his doubts and fears had come down. He found himself sweating profusely the cold, ill-smelling sweat of anxiety and fear.

The technician finished removing the cast and led Tony down a corridor to the X-ray department. It seemed a long way. Tony, on crutches, was tired and impatient by the time they arrived; it had been only minutes. He could almost feel the anxiety affecting his perceptions. He wanted to go home, to be alone; he was thirsty.

The X-rays were taken.

Tony's appointment with the doctor was not for three days. Three more days of waiting. They did not go by easily.

And then the doctor said neither yes nor no. Tony felt, on that day, he could have lived with either. But there was to be nothing so definite. He sat in the same office in Boca Raton, where this had all begun. Across from him, behind the desk, sat the same doctor who, months before, had told him he might yet lose what remained of his foot; but there had been one chance. . .now the new X-rays were clipped to the viewer. The doctor motioned toward them as he began to speak.

"I'd like to be able to say it's a hundred percent success, Tony," the doctor said, "but I can't. We've gained some, the angle is definitely better. But if it's enough? I just can't say, for sure."

Tony's mouth formed itself into a line. His eyes became wet.

"We're going to have to leave the final word to the prosthetics people; they'll know best if you can be fitted. . .I'm sorry, Tony. I wish I had something better to tell you."

Tony nodded.

"I've got you an appointment at Jackson Memorial Hospital in Miami," the doctor said. "It's a veterans hospital. They have their own prosthetics department. They're very good at this sort of thing."

"How soon?" Tony asked softly.

"Next week, Thursday," the doctor said.

144

"Could it be sooner?"

"It's the earliest I could get. I had to collect a favor to do that."

Tony nodded. "All right," he said.

"Do you want something? I could write you a prescription for a mild tranquilizer—to help with the waiting?"

Tony shook his head. There was a moment's silence.

"Good luck, Tony," the doctor said, and offered his hand. "I'll be in touch with Jackson Memorial after your appointment. I hope like hell I don't have to see you again."

They shook hands.

More waiting. Tony's feelings oscillated wildly. He wondered how many times he could go up and down. It seemed he could not go on hoping much longer. At times he felt he would have preferred that the operation be a clear failure. At least then there would have been an end to the uncertainty. He had not been prepared to extend the waiting. *Yes* or *no!* He wanted an answer. But there was none, not yet.

Tony wanted someone to be angry at. Someone to blame. But there was no one. Not even the original doctor who had left him half a foot: it still might turn out to be best. Tony could feel no malice toward his present doctor; he had been honest from the start. And he obviously cared. Tony's anxiety was not focused against anything—which made it all the harder to bear.

He was like a man at sea, lost in a fog: drifting, where? There was no way to know.

Tony's first trip to Jackson Memorial Hospital clarified nothing. The prosthetist who examined him echoed the doctor: it was neither yes nor no. They could try, that was all. And there was to be more waiting, four more weeks while his prosthesis was built.

Tony waited. He managed to work, and he continued to see a few friends. But he mostly waited. He stayed on his crutches, not wanting to reopen his wound. His stump was completely healed, the best it had been since the accident. Tony wanted it that way to try the prosthesis.

The four weeks of waiting made it September, September 1973, a year and three months from the time of the accident. And he was to wear a prosthesis for the very first time.

He arrived at the hospital to pick up his prosthesis on the appointed day, and was taken to a physical therapy room. Full-length mirrors covered the walls. A few chairs were clustered near the door, and a set of parallel bars filled the center of the room.

The same prosthetist Tony had seen on his first visit soon entered, prosthesis in hand. It looked like a white plastic boot with the topside cut away; a hard, black rubber toepiece was attached at the arch. The prosthetist handed it to Tony and took a step back. Tony turned it over in his hands, fascinated. It was not what he had expected. He really didn't know what he had expected—but it wasn't this.

"It's a bit of an experiment," the prosthetist said; "you've a very unusual amputation."

Tony stood with the prosthesis in his hands, feeling anxious and awkward. He didn't know what to say or do.

"Well," said the prosthetist, finally, "shall we give it a try?" He motioned toward a chair. Tony nodded and sat down.

The prosthetist slipped a light sock, and then a heavier one, for cushion, over Tony's stump; then the prosthesis: Tony's heel was fit snuggly into place, bringing the back of the prosthesis up to cradle his calf. The plastic felt cool against his leg.

The prosthetist brought out a pair of heavy black shoes; the left shoe was a size larger than the right. He put these, with the aid of a shoehorn, onto Tony's feet. He helped Tony up and led him to the parallel bars. And Tony was walking. Not well, and it hurt a great deal. But he was walking!

In the excitement of the moment Tony overlooked every negative sign. He clumped up and down between the parallel bars, and grinned at the prosthetist. The prosthetist stood back, eyeing things critically. "We'll have to see," he said, "we'll have to see."

But Tony was in no mood to be discouraged. He was sure that with practice he could learn to walk perfectly. And he could bear the pain; perhaps it would even cease, as his phantom pains had ceased. He left the hospital in high spirits, already thinking that he would bring his father to this place. Perhaps they could help him too.

Tony's mood was soon dampened. The next day when he got down to serious walking, he could see that his clumsiness involved more than just lack of practice. Up and back, over and over, he walked the length of his bedroom. He was still coming down on the end of his stump. Not as badly as before, he told himself; he was no longer hop walking as he had with the shoe mold—he was walking better than at any other time since his accident. He pressed on, no longer euphoric, but still encouraged.

The following day the pain in his stump became severe. He tried to explain it away, concluding that he was overdoing the practice; a more gradual approach was needed. He cut down the time he wore the prosthesis, using his crutches a part of each day. The pain continued. Then, on the fifth day of use, the prosthesis cracked down the

147

back; it split where it supported his heel—and became useless.

Tony did not brood. He sensed that he must maintain the forward momentum he had established. He had to stay on his feet. The prosthesis must be repaired. He returned to Miami and met with the prosthetist who had fitted him.

"I was afraid of this," the prosthetist said, after examining the broken prosthesis. "You're not going to like this, but I'm afraid the only real solution is a conventional below-knee limb. . .that means a standard amputation."

Tony was struck in the face with the fear which had haunted him for almost seven months now, ever since the first mention of another amputation. He rebelled instantly.

"We didn't give it a fair try," he said. "Can't you fix it, beef it up a little, maybe?"

The prosthetist turned the prosthesis over in his hands. He placed it in an upright position on the floor and pressed down, approximating the stress of walking. He looked doubtful.

Tony was silent, waiting.

The prosthetist sighed. "I'll try," he said, "but I can't promise a thing."

"How long?" Tony asked. "Is there any chance you could work on it right away?" Tony was pressing. He was grateful that this man was even trying to help him. But he could not be patient, not anymore.

The prosthetist seemed to understand. "Soon as I can," he said.

Tony received a call the next day. The prosthetist had stayed up most of the night, working. It was finished. Tony drove immediately back to Miami.

The prosthesis had been remade in a thicker plastic.

And straps, to hold the back more firmly in place, had been added. "It's all I know to do," the prosthetist seemed almost to apologize. "I hope it works." Tony thanked him.

The new prosthesis was stiff and exaggerated the clumsiness of Tony's walk. And the pain in his stump resumed and grew steadily worse. During the second week that he wore it ulcerations began to form on the end of his stump. Soon the wound was reopened and oozing.

Tony refused to admit the prosthesis had failed. He continued to use it, blindly determined to make it work. The alternative loomed like an ever-increasing shadow across his mind. Without realizing, he was running away. He stayed on his feet for hours at a time, fanatically ignoring the pain. His walk grew more and more clumsy, as the sores on his stump worsened. Infection set in. Still Tony pressed himself to walk.

Then the prosthesis broke. It cracked and split, exactly as the one before it.

It was over.

The alternative remained. Tony knew it too well. He had lived with it now for almost a year; and, dwelling within him, it had grown more and more terrible. In his mind's eye he could see, almost feel, what remained of his foot being cut away: his ankle, gone—his new stump, on a line from his knee.

Tony had thought he was ready to accept this, as an alternative to waiting, a dozen times. He had felt he could not possibly face it, a dozen more. And now he found himself caught in between, immobilized by what he tried to tell himself was an irrational fear. He was unable to move, putting off all appointments with the doctor and then castigating himself for his cowardice.

He sat and brooded. All of the medical and prosthetic

advice was the same: a below-knee amputation, and all would be fine. *All would be fine.* He had heard that before. The doctor who had told him to put paper in his shoe had used similar words. Why should he believe them? Why should he go through the ordeal of another amputation and end up the same? Perhaps worse. How many times could you be expected to believe? He had gained and lost faith, both in others and himself, so many times.

But what choice was there? Live the rest of his life on crutches, or in a wheelchair? This did not seem an impossible choice, not anymore. At least he would be off this merry-go-round of false hope. Tony found himself wishing, ironically, that his foot had been another few inches under the train—that the decision had been made for him. Tony wondered, even if he *knew* what to do, whether he would have the strength left to do it.

17

The telephone in the Black Road apartment was ringing. Bill had just come home from his office and was sitting with the day's mail at a coffee table in the living room. Dojna was not yet home. A maid was fixing supper in the kitchen. She answered the phone.

"For you, Mr. Barr," she said, appearing in the living room archway. "It's your son."

Bill rose awkwardly from his chair. His mouth was set in a line: a mixture of impatience and pain. "I'll take it in the den, May, thank you," he said, and walked slowly from the room, his mouth still set, still looking away. He was wearing his prosthesis and limped very badly: a lurching, unsteady gait that filled his stump with pain on each step.

In the den he closed the door behind him and allowed his face to relax. A look of pain spread quickly over his features. Walking even such very short distances was an ordeal. He did not look well at all. He hesitated a moment, gathering himself, and then picked up the phone; his voice was steady. His greeting to Tony conveyed an impression of strength that he in no way felt.

Bill listened intently to the latest events in Tony's story: the broken prosthesis, the pain. Tony's speech was thick and slow, he had been drinking; he seemed to have reached the end of all hope. Bill understood all too well.

Silently, as he listened, tears came to Bill's eyes—they were for himself, as well as for Tony. Bill could not clearly distinguish between Tony's feelings and his own. It seemed he and Tony were caught in the same nightmare, being punished by God for some family sin that Bill could not comprehend. Against his own will, Bill searched for that sin—within himself, within the past.

Visions of his father, and the unbridled political power he had wielded, filled Bill's mind; and Bill's own bouts with alcohol; his divorces; his problems with Tony as a boy. And then the bombing, the sudden flash of flame and thunder, and pain, came into Bill's mind; *the bombing*, still unsolved—his tormentor unpunished while he suffered. Bill pulled himself instinctively away from these images: a whirlpool within himself that he must not fall into.

Bill felt tired, so very tired. As he listened to Tony, his own story began to run through his mind. Especially the events of late. While Tony had waited to undergo his heel-cord surgery, Bill had been at the medical center at Duke University.

Duke University, at first, had proved to be more of the same. Neuromas were diagnosed. Cortisone shots were prescribed. Bill was passed from doctor to doctor and heard nothing new.

Then he was told he should have a new prosthesis.

In the past, most doctors had not even inspected his prosthesis. It usually sat in a corner while he was examined. Most prosthetic advice he had sought on his own. But Duke University had its own prosthetic department, and one of the doctors prescribed a new leg for Bill. Bill remembered the words of an earlier doctor—"the source of your pain is either in your body or your mind or your prosthesis. . . ." Bill was glad to have a doctor interested in the prosthesis. The Duke prosthetic department was clean and appeared modern—a vivid contrast to the many

152

other prosthetic facilities Bill had visited. He was encouraged.

This was to be Bill's sixth leg: two had been constructed at the firm he had visited directly after the bombing, the second of these he still wore; then came the leg prescribed by Mayo Clinic, built at the firm in Minneapolis; the strap leg, his own idea, had come next; and finally the fifth prosthesis—the worst of the lot—had been built by a firm in Chicago. Duke University now built Bill his sixth prosthesis.

He wore it less than a week and left it behind in his hotel room. Another failure.

Next, Bill had gone to Doctor's Hospital in Washington, D. C. The amputation of Teddy Kennedy Jr.'s leg had been much in the news. At Doctor's Hospital, Bill sought out the surgeon the Kennedys had selected. Surely they had gone to the best.

Neuromas were again diagnosed. But this time with a different solution. Instead of attempting to remove the neuromas, as had been tried at Mayo Clinic, it was suggested the sciatic nerve in Bill's stump be severed. The transmission of pain from the stump to the spine and ultimately to the brain would be largely reduced, the doctor had said.

Bill had the operation, his third since the bombing. The surgery was beautifully performed. Hope had run high: the famous doctor, the famous hospital. . .but it had come to nothing. The pain in Bill's stump continued. After, it was hard for him to fathom how he had once again *believed* so strongly that he was going to be helped.

But back in Joliet he heard of yet another procedure and found himself hoping, if not believing, again. This time a lumbar block—a spinal injection to deaden the nerves which ran to his stump.

Bill located a doctor in Chicago who would administer the treatment. The appointment was arranged. He was given his first lumbar block as an outpatient in a Chicago hospital and, with no observation period, released.

During the drive home he suffered severe chest pains and began to cough violently: the doctor had pierced one of his lungs with the injection needle. Fortunately, Dojna had been with him. She rushed him back to the hospital. . .

A few weeks later, recovered from this complication, Bill scheduled an appointment for another lumbar block—this time at the University of Illinois Pain Clinic. He was determined to give this form of treatment a chance: the first lumbar block had not failed, the doctor administering it had. Bill was still determined, still able to reason—but it was becoming increasingly difficult.

The pain in his stump was unrelenting, it seemed to grow even worse as his hope lessened. His general mistrust of the medical profession was turning to fear, bordering at times on delusions of persecution. He wanted to withdraw from the world, to hide. His feelings were much like those he had had in 1972, just before he attempted suicide—they frightened him. But he fought against them; he kept on.

At the University of Illinois Pain Clinic, the doctors were expert at administering lumbar blocks, and the initial results were encouraging. After the first block was given, Bill's pain was significantly reduced—numbed as with cortisone shots, only more so. But this lasted only a matter of hours. Precious hours, after nearly *four years* of constant pain: so soon they were gone.

A second lumbar block produced similar results, but the period of relief was even less. And soon the blocks lost their effect entirely. Bill's hopes had once again been lifted, only to shatter.

Near desperation, Bill visited another surgeon, a consultant to professional athletic teams, a man who had much experience with pain. Bill almost begged him to take away his suffering. The surgeon told him of two possibilities—two operations. The first was a *gangrectomy*: the nerves connecting Bill's stump and his brain would be severed at the central relay point within his spine. He would emerge from the operation with no feeling at all in his leg, and probably would be unable to use a prosthesis: he would be confined to a wheelchair for the rest of his life. There was also a high risk he would lose control of his bowels and urine and be permanently incapable of achieving an erection. The other possibility was the implantation of an electrode in Bill's brain, to short-circuit the transmission of pain from his stump. This procedure was very new, unperfected, the side effects were virtually unknown—the surgeon could not recommend it.

Bill debated long himself. A wheelchair, without pain, he could have accepted. But the rest, he wasn't ready to accept the rest—not yet.

His search for help seemed in vain, but he would not quit. Perhaps because he knew the alternative—he had tasted the ashes of attempting to take his own life. But it was more than that too. It was his oath to help Tony, and others. And it was something inside himself he could not tame, something he had almost thrown away when he had laid down his will and attempted to die—something he valued all the more for that experience.

He continued his search: chiropractors, osteopaths, physiatrists, more surgeons; biofeedback, nutrition. . .it all ran together in his mind, back to his attempted suicide and then back beyond that to the mayoral campaign and the bombing itself. There had been three operations, a psychiatrist, a half-dozen artificial limbs being padded and shimmed and adjusted. Bill could no longer recite all the things he had tried, nor could he keep track of the times. One doctor had even called him a *manchusion*—a highly skilled, pathological faker of illness—and had threatened to put his name on a list that was circulated to warn other doctors and hospitals of such people. Still, Bill would not quit. He got up each day and kept on.

And now Tony's call. Bill reminded himself brutally of his oath to find help, and it seemed, at this moment, a shallow act of arrogance. He was filled with feelings of powerlessness and sorrow. But even now, he would not quit.

In desperation he told Tony to come to Joliet. They would go to the firm where Bill's first two prostheses had been built—Bill could at least walk on the limbs he had had made there; perhaps not well, but at least he could walk. Perhaps they could help Tony, too. It was desperate. But out of all Bill's searching, it was the best he could offer.

Tony was hesitant. "I don't know, Dad," he said, "I don't know if I have it to try anymore. . .maybe I should just let them cut off the rest of my foot and be done with it. Maybe I just won't do anything. . .that seems simplest. I'm so tired. . ."

"Tony," Bill said, "don't quit. Have the foot off, or come here; or go somewhere else—but decide! Don't drift, that's suicide. *I know.*"

Tony was silent. They had been talking a very long time.

"All right, Dad," he said finally. "All right, I'll come." But there was no conviction in his voice. No will of his own. Bill sensed that he himself had become the strongest force acting on Tony, and that that was why Tony was coming—not because he had made a decision. Tony was drifting. And it scared the hell out of Bill.

Part Three

1974–

18

Jan had returned to Michigan, to prosthetics. He had moved the Stokosa practice from Jackson to Lansing, the state capital, to be nearer a newly formed group of orthopedic surgeons. His brother-in-law, who had been running the practice, elected to take a position elsewhere.

The group of surgeons was highly progressive; among their goals was a greater knowledge of prosthetics. Jan had previously worked with one of the surgeons and had been invited to be a consultant. He advised the surgeons of the prosthetic implications of the various amputations which they performed. This was an unusual relationship for surgeon and prosthetist. It implied a gap in the surgeon's knowledge, a gap few surgeons were willing to acknowledge.

Jan was pleased with the progress of this experiment. It was the kind of new professional ground he wanted to break. But it was an isolated bright spot. On other fronts, he was meeting determined resistance.

In the state and national prosthetic associations Jan

found his ideas engendered hostility, a response he did not at first understand. Finally, an older prosthetist from Detroit took Jan aside and explained...

Jan was advocating increased education and more rigorous certification for prosthetists. He speculated that few outside the profession understood that a certified prosthetist was required to have only eighteen weeks of specialized academic preparation. Jan was pushing the ideas of required seminars for practicing prosthetists, and the revamping of educational requirements for prosthetists of the future. He felt the prerequisites for certification should be at least as rigorous as those for other skilled professionals.

In addition, Jan advocated some type of third-party control for the field of prosthetics. The prosthetics industry was completely self-regulated. It seemed a third party, as in law and medicine, should be involved to protect the public interest. A state test perhaps, which, along with cementing the higher proposed academic standards and imposing greater control on the existing apprenticeship programs, would keep individuals with no objective qualifications from practicing.

Further, Jan spoke against what he called the "assembly-line mentality" prevalent in prosthetics. He maintained that every limb should be a separate creation, suited to the individual and his lifestyle.

Jan attributed assembly-line thinking in prosthetics largely to government agencies like the Veteran's Administration and to insurance companies. Government healthcare plans along with insurance companies paid ninety percent of all prosthetic bills and were using their powerful position with the industry to hold prices artificially low. They refused, in many cases, to pay for the more advanced prosthetic technology, and they demanded across-the-board prices rather than a case-by-case determination. This, Jan argued, put economic pressure on the prosthetist to use the cheapest possible methods and materials—to mass-produce limbs; all of which would keep standards of comparison, within the industry, artificially low.

Jan suggested that when the VA, for instance, demanded an across-the-board price for a below-knee prosthesis, prosthetists should in an organized fashion refuse: no limb would be quoted without first examining the amputee who was to wear it. Ultimately, this would create a broader range of pricing and allow the individual prosthetist to utilize the more advanced technology and, where warranted, the more time-consuming and expensive prosthetic techniques. The individual prosthetist could then make a quality limb, suited to the individual, and still stay in business.

The prosthetist as well as the individual amputee would become a part of the prescription process. They would gain a say in determining the amputee's prosthetic needs—instead of having it all economically predetermined at the barest level by an anonymous bureaucrat. Jan felt very strongly about this.

Finally, Jan felt something needed to be done about the doctor-prosthetist relationship. According to the ethics of the national prosthetic association, to which he belonged, no prosthetist should construct a limb without a prescription from a doctor. And yet doctors, by and large, knew next to nothing about prosthetics.

Often, even the surgeons who did amputations regularly were not well acquainted with the more advanced prosthetic technology. How could they possibly properly prepare the amputee's body for the prosthesis. Lines of communication between doctor and prosthetist had to be opened.

Jan held out the experimental project he was presently involved with as at least a partial, temporary solution. But in the long run, after the field of prosthetics was upgraded, shouldn't the prosthetist prescribe for himself? Does a dentist ask a medical doctor to prescribe for *his* patients? Prosthetists were no longer just carpenters fashioning a peg. The field had grown up, and it was time for those in it to grow up too. Strong words from a prosthetist so young, but then few knew the price Jan had paid in earning his right to say them. As much as anyone else's, prosthetics was *his* field. Since the age of seven it had been his life.

Jan felt he had a well-thought-out position. He had spent a great deal of time and energy preparing it; along with his patients, it was the central focus of his life. He had not expected that his ideas would be quickly or easily accepted. It was to him only a starting point in the process of much-needed change. He was prepared for people to disagree, for a give and take. But the hostility he encountered took him by surprise.

The older prosthetist from Detroit—who privately agreed with many of Jan's ideas—explained. He pointed out Jan's blind spot. Jan had been looking at the whole problem from the point of view of the amputee and the prosthetist—he had not considered the owners of the large prosthetic establishments and prosthetic chains. This relatively small group of men employed large stables of prosthetists and technicians, and turned out large numbers of artificial limbs. These owners were also, by and large, the officers of the professional prosthetic associations. And they were the ones, Jan's adviser pointed out, who stood to lose by Jan's suggestions.

"First of all," said the older prosthetist, "if the education and training of prosthetists were upgraded, status and potential earnings would also rise. This would attract more talented individuals to the profession and increase the market value of those already in it. Prosthetists would likely begin to act independently, like other professionals, opening their own offices *and* no longer remain willing to be the 'cash cows' of the owners."

As for Jan's idea of state or some other type of third-party control, the older prosthetist had to laugh: "Does anyone really want to be controlled?" he said.

"But we already are," Jan said, "if we want to get *certified*—and stay that way."

"*You* are," corrected the older prosthetist; "the owners are in political control of the certifying and regulating bodies—the professional associations. The *owners* control *themselves*."

He continued: "Look at what you're suggesting from their point of view. If you own a large firm and have effective regulatory control over your widespread but smaller competition, you control the organizations which make the rules which govern their professional lives—let alone the fact that you have the luxury of regulating your own life—do you want to give that up to a third party?" He laughed again.

"But a small operator can belong to the associations," Jan protested.

"Technically, yes," said the older prosthetist, "but how many of the small operators can afford the travel or the time off to effectively participate? And even if they could, do you think they could make a dent in the united front of the big boys?"

Jan had to be silent on both counts: he could not really

afford his association involvement, and he had not been able to make even the slightest dent.

"Jan," the older prosthetist said, "this third-party control is no simple issue. As a prosthetist, I'm not sure I'm ready to trade in the 'owners' for the government."

"But as an amputee, what would you want?" Jan asked.

The older prosthetist was silent, unconvinced but thoughtful. "It's not right the way it is," he said finally, "I'll agree to that."

Jan was slowly learning about the political and financial realities of life. He found himself wondering if perhaps Walter had not once learned these same lessons. Perhaps Walter had tried to bring about change, failed; and withdrew to create a professional island, on which to practice his own brand of prosthetics and to train his son. These thoughts explained a great many things.

And the older prosthetist from Detroit, Jan's adviser—he had the look and sound of a man who had once tried to change things too.

The older prosthetist had one more thing to tell Jan, a warning: "Remember," he said, "the big boys control your certification and the certification of your facility. Don't get them too angry with you. And *don't* antagonize doctors or the VA—they're your bread and butter."

But Jan was in no mood for temperate advice.

Joliet, the Black Road apartment. Bill sat alone in the den. He sat very quietly. It was late afternoon, just turning dark outside. He made no move to turn on a light as the darkness settled around him.

It was two days since Tony had left Joliet. It seemed like a dream, unreal, that Tony had been there at all. Bill and Tony had gone through the motions of having Tony

163

fitted with a new prosthesis, neither really believing it would work, each trying to hide this feeling from the other. Tony had been blasé, distant, locked in a private world that he allowed no one to enter. Bill had been manic, talking incessantly, trying to convince Tony, and himself, that they *must* hope; he had insisted they go out to dinners, which nobody tasted; he had made jokes, but the laughter was strained. And his own feelings of hopelessness, underneath the mask he wore, deepened severely.

The new prosthesis was inferior, even at first sight, to the ones Tony already had. The footpiece was similar, but there was no back piece at all; the device depended on the ankle for its total support. Tony's walk was nearly as poor as with the shoe mold or with the newspaper packed in the toe of his shoe.

Tony made a feeble attempt, for Bill's sake, to pretend the new prosthesis might work. But it was so obviously inadequate that he soon dropped the pose.

Before returning to Florida, Tony tried to thank his father for trying to help him, tried to say something to make Bill feel better, less responsible—but he could not find the words. Bill could find no words either. Dojna cautioned Tony to take better care of the ulcerations on his stump. During his stay Dojna had bathed and treated the ulcerations several times daily; she feared a serious infection. Tony nodded mechanically to this advice. There were awkward hugs and handshakes, and then Tony was boarding his plane.

Bill and Dojna watched Tony walk from sight—his limp was as bad as Bill's, perhaps worse.

Now, sitting alone, it was hard for Bill to believe this had really taken place: almost the way shock makes things seem unreal, as if they were being imagined or happening to someone else.

Bill thought back to the time right after Tony's accident. There had been questions about Tony's care, even then—but no solutions. Bill remembered a discussion he had had with Dojna. . .

"Do you think we should get Tony to another hospital, get him a new doctor?" Bill had asked.

Dojna had looked thoughtful, worried. Bill could still see her in his mind's eye weighing the question. "Bill," she had said, "it would be next to impossible to find a surgeon who would take over the case at this stage—these relationships, between surgeons, are very delicate."

"Damn these doctors and their delicate relationships!" Bill had said. He had been impatient and dissatisfied with Tony's treatment. But he had had no real grounds for complaint.

Dojna had read his feelings. "The care at this little hospital has been excellent," she had said. "I've talked a great deal with Tony's doctor, he's trying to save as much of the foot as possible. . .I'm convinced he's doing what he thinks is best."

"But does he know what he's doing?"

"Bill, that I don't know. I'm not a surgeon. I don't perform amputations. I know very little about this specialty."

"I know, Dojna. I'm sorry," Bill had said. "I expect you to be everything. I'm sorry."

Save as much of the foot as possible. And now Tony faced a second amputation, and he had lost nearly two years of his life. Bill sat in the gathering darkness and fought down an anger that threatened to consume him.

Dojna came quietly into the den and turned on a lamp.

She sat down in a chair beside Bill. They sat quietly for a time. And then Bill began to speak, almost to himself.

"I don't want to quit," he said. He sounded far away, exhausted. "I don't want to but I just don't know. . .I don't know if I can do it anymore. I don't believe anymore, Dojna. . .I don't believe it's ever going to end. I've lost it. . ."

Dojna took Bill's hand, quieting him. She had watched Bill go up and come down on this psychological roller coaster before. She understood the dangers. But where was the alternative?

There was no *adjustment* to constant pain at this level, one either fought it actively or succumbed to it. And there was no *adjustment* to having one's son lost in a maze of terrifying decisions, not knowing yourself which way he should turn, or if there was a way. How was a man to *adjust* to that?

Dojna did not question Bill. She stood by him, and with him, as she had done from the beginning. She was the one he could turn to for comfort and support. And she provided a reality outside himself, a reality he believed in and trusted. Dojna understood this and accepted it, knowing full well the impossible responsibility she carried, and feeling its weight. But again, with the events since the bombing as prologue, where was the alternative?

Often, she had sat with Bill, talking late into the evening, he putting off going to bed, dreading the drug-induced nightmare half sleep that filled his nights, the nausea when he woke; she understanding this, pushing back her own need for sleep to be with him. They talked about Tony, and they tried to sort out the latest medical advice Bill had been given. Forever, it seemed, this had been their life. And Dojna had accepted it, lived with it, taken her role as best she could understand it—supporting Bill, never leading him.

But now it was different. Dojna had watched Bill slipping, in the days since Tony's visit. She had listened to his voice growing fainter, even as he tried to rally himself. She watched his strength slipping away, being consumed by the final stages of exhaustion and depression. It was time she must act.

"Bill," she said, "I pray you don't misunderstand me, but I must tell you, I must tell you. Bill, I think it is time you should see a psychiatrist."

Bill was wounded; it spread over his face like a shadow, the look Dojna had anticipated, dreaded. Had she finally come to doubt him too?

"No, no, Bill," she said, tightening her hand over his, "I *know* that your pain is real. But you need help, help with your struggle."

His face softened.

"I know a man," she said, "a man whose judgment I trust, a psychiatrist. I believe he will understand your condition; I believe he will know what to do—not for your leg but for your *will*. I believe he can help you continue to fight."

Bill and Dojna sat in the waiting room of Alex J. Spadoni, M.D., professor of clinical psychiatry at the Loyola Medical School, president of the Illinois Psychiatric Society. The credentials did not impress Bill. He had seen too many doctors by now for that. It was Dojna's faith in this man that gave Bill any inkling of hope.

Bill and Dojna went together into Dr. Spadoni's inner office. It was very businesslike, well organized and neat. Dr. Spadoni wore a three-piece suit and sat at a large desk made of metal and glass.

Dojna made the introductions. It was clear that she and Dr. Spadoni knew each other, but there was no feeling of collaboration. Dojna had advised Bill to come here, she had made the appointment—she had even guessed what Dr. Spadoni might do. But she would not involve herself in any clinical aspect of this meeting. She was Bill's wife; and she understood that this, above all else, was what Bill needed from her. She had known this from the beginning. She had chosen Dr. Spadoni. Now she must trust him.

Dr. Spadoni seemed to sense Dojna's position, and he interacted directly with Bill.

Bill told his story, as he had told it now so many times. Dr. Spadoni listened intently, making notes from time to time.

After Bill had finished, Dr. Spadoni asked several questions. He was particularly interested in Bill's reactions to

Elavil, the antidepressant drug Bill had been given in 1971.

Dr. Spadoni wrote out a prescription. "Ordinarily," he said, "I'd have you hospitalized while we try this. There are sometimes side effects—but I think Dojna can watch for those." He turned to Dojna. She nodded.

Dr. Spadoni handed the prescription to Bill. "I think this will get the adrenalin flowing, Bill," he said, "get you back to normal."

That was it. The appointment lasted less than an hour. The drug Bill was to take was *parnaide*. . .

Three days later, at seven o'clock in the morning, Bill was up and shaving. He noticed it was spring. Outside the bathroom window, the trees were already in full leaf. Three days before, he hadn't noticed. His leg hurt as always. But he was up, and he noticed the spring.

He felt not changed but returned to himself. The gathering cloud of hopelessness and persecution had lifted. He was ready, once more, to face the world; to resume his search for help. It was much like waking from a dream. Dr. Spadoni, at least through Bill's eyes, had performed a miracle. Bill was deeply grateful.

Dr. Spadoni was to do one more thing for Bill, a thing which, up to now, Bill's most determined efforts had been unable to achieve—he arranged, for Bill, an appointment with Dr. Howard Kurland.

Dr. Howard Kurland was a man well acquainted with pain. He had personally suffered for many years with lower back pain caused by a herniated disk. Surgery, for a number of complicated medical reasons, was inadvisable. Other forms of treatment had consistently failed.

Searching for relief, Dr. Kurland had gone to mainland China to learn about acupuncture. He was relieved of his pain, and stayed on to learn its use. Returning to the United States, he married this new knowledge with Western medical thinking and technology.

Dojna heard Dr. Kurland speak at a medical conference. She was skeptical about his ideas. But she, like Bill, was leaving no stone unturned. She was investigating every form of treatment that showed even the slightest promise.

Dr. Kurland was used to skeptics. The talk Dojna attended was late in the afternoon, after a full day of meetings. Dr. Kurland asked if anyone present had a headache. Several did, including an acquaintance of Dojna's. Dr. Kurland brought these people forward and gave them relief—using a finger-pressure technique based on the principles of acupuncture.

The skepticism reduced, Dr. Kurland proceeded with his lecture. Dojna was impressed. Even though Bill had already undergone acupuncture, she felt that with Dr. Kurland it was worth another try.

Dojna had tried to get Bill an appointment, with no success. Dr. Kurland was in high demand. He was scheduled almost a year in advance and was not seeing new patients. Bill had tried to get an appointment through influential friends. But no appointment had materialized. Bill continued his efforts; but the more he persisted the tighter the door seemed to close. Dr. Kurland would not see him, period.

Finally, with Tony's visit, and the subsequent deepening of Bill's depression, all efforts to see Dr. Kurland had ceased. Along with everything else, it had seemed futile.

But now, Bill was back on his feet. Once again, he sought an appointment. And Dr. Spadoni was able to open the door.

Bill drove alone to Evanston, Illinois, to see Dr. Kurland, the first time in over a year he had felt confident to travel without Dojna. His appointment was in the evening, after the regular office hours.

Bill found the address, an older building, large, with many names on a glass-encased list near the door. He found Dr. Kurland's name and an office number. The building was unlocked.

The lights in the hallway were dimmed. Bill's steps echoed loudly. An old-fashioned elevator, complete with metal gate, took him up several floors. The elevator hummed.

Dr. Kurland's waiting room was empty. Bill passed through it and knocked on the door of the inner office.

"Yes, all right, come in." The voice sounded impatient. Bill opened the door.

Dr. Kurland sat behind a huge mahogany desk, a small, well-dressed man with sharp features. The office was luxurious, even by famous-doctor standards: overstuffed leather sofa and chairs; paintings; a dark, textured carpet. A small lamp on Dr. Kurland's desk lighted the room. He was signing papers, which he finished while Bill stood and waited. Finally he looked up.

"Sit down, Mr. Barr," he said, motioning toward the sofa. He waited until Bill was seated and then looked at him squarely. "I don't like the way you've pushed to get this appointment."

Bill said nothing.

"It's going to be eighty dollars."

Bill shrugged: that was all right.

"What's wrong?" Dr. Kurland asked.

Bill told his story. Responding to Dr. Kurland's mood, he told it briefly, skipping over much of the nearly five years since the bombing. Dr. Kurland interrupted only once, to ask questions about Bill's previous experience with acupuncture.

"Well, then, let's see what we can do," Dr. Kurland said when Bill had finished; his tone was now matter of fact, no longer angry. He came around his desk; and, from a cabinet, took a jumble of wires and electronic-looking devices and placed them on a coffee table in front of Bill.

Dr. Kurland attached a dull metal probe, by means of one of the wires, to a meter. For several minutes he touched the probe to various points on, and inside of, Bill's ears.

When this was finished, he sat down in the chair nearest Bill. His tone was entirely changed.

"How many times have you attempted suicide?" he asked.

Dr. Kurland's insight took Bill by surprise. But he answered directly.

"Just once, in 1972. But I've thought about it, a lot."

Dr. Kurland nodded his head. "Mr. Barr," he said, "you're a pretty tough guy—your total nervous system, every circuit in your body, is completely disrupted. I'm surprised you're here."

Bill's face was flushed—to have the reality of his pain confirmed after so many had doubted it was almost overwhelming. "How can you tell this?" he asked.

"There are a number of nervous systems," Dr. Kurland explained, his manner and tone no longer brusque, "all of them interrelated. The electrical impulses generated by these systems are visible through my instruments. I can guess the intensity of your pain by observing its effects on the furthest-removed system—somewhat as you could judge the size of a rock dropped in a pond by observing the ripples."

Bill nodded.

Dr. Kurland looked directly at Bill, for a long moment, an understanding look—he too had suffered.

Bill realized that Dr. Kurland was a man of great complexity; concerned, warm, perhaps even shy—not at all as he had seemed at first. Dr. Kurland had probably judged Bill's persistent efforts to see him as a millionaire's obsession, a neurotic intrusion on his already overloaded schedule; perhaps he had even been warned by other Chicago area doctors that Bill was a professional patient. Whatever the reasons, it had been quite clear at the outset that Dr. Kurland was seeing Bill *only* as a favor to Dr. Spadoni.

But now Dr. Kurland understood Bill's persistence for what it had been: desperation and need. The physician in Dr. Kurland was fully awakened, his concentration now focused completely on Bill.

Tiny pins were inserted, by Dr. Kurland, into Bill's ears; there was no pain, nor did Bill's ears bleed even slightly. The pins were attached by wires to a black metal box with gauges and dials.

Dr. Kurland adjusted the dials, asking Bill to report when he felt the slightest vibration. Bill nodded when this occurred.

Dr. Kurland now asked Bill how his stump felt. Bill frowned, almost unsure of his own perceptions.

"Warm," he said, finally, hesitantly, "almost like there's a hot-water bottle on it—it usually feels cold."

"Ah, good," said Dr. Kurland, smiling, "we have circulation." He continued to adjust the dials.

The feeling in Bill's stump changed gradually to numbness, as it had felt at first with cortisone shots and lumbar blocks. This feeling soon passed. The pain seemed to grow faint: like the morphine effect, Bill thought, remembering

173

his first days in the hospital after the bombing. Then the pain suddenly faded completely away. Bill felt momentarily nauseated and blacked out.

He woke to find Dr. Kurland taking his pulse. A blood-pressure cuff was attached to his arm, the pins in his ears were gone.

"You're fine," Dr. Kurland assured him. "You simply passed out for a while. How does your stump feel?"

"I can feel some pain, not bad, though," Bill said. "What happened? The pain was gone. . ."

"Yes, I know," said Dr. Kurland. He smiled. "Your system has lived with pain for so long that it responds upside down. You passed out from *shock*—the shock of having no pain."

Bill sank back into his chair. "Oh, my God," he said. And he prayed he wasn't dreaming.

20

Dr. Kurland explained to Bill that the pain in his stump would gradually return. A series of treatments would be required to eliminate it completely. Unfortunately, Dr. Kurland was leaving for a two-month stay on mainland China. Bill would have to wait.

Bill left Dr. Kurland's office nearly free of pain. Almost holding his breath, he prayed, with each step, that the pain would not suddenly return—that this was not all a dream. By the time he arrived home, he was beginning to believe what had happened was real.

That night Bill slept soundly. It was the best sleep he had had since the bombing. He woke the next morning with little pain, and a new level of energy and optimism.

He went to his office and found himself able to concentrate, he could grasp things quickly and thoroughly; this felt, at first, strange and new, then rediscovered—like a blurred image brought suddenly into focus. Bill took joy in his ability to work.

By noon, he had accomplished a great deal. He had been physically very active and his stump began to hurt.

He remained optimistic. The pain did not approach its previous level; but more than that, he *believed* he was going to be helped. Dr. Kurland would return from China and the pain would be taken away. This belief made all the difference. Bill felt he could suffer almost anything if he knew there was help up ahead.

The following day was a Saturday. Bill played gin rummy with a group of close friends—a favorite pastime, all but forgotten. There were a few moments of awkward silence, until Senator Benedict (Sparky) Garmisa bemoaned Bill's return to the world of gin rummy, saying his own secret hopes to be world champion were now dashed. This broke the silence with laughter. And if not just like old times, still the afternoon was wonderful. To be living and not just existing: Bill savored each moment.

Bill and Dojna ate a quiet dinner, that night, in a Joliet restaurant. Neither mentioned Bill's leg for the entire evening: an unspoken agreement between them. They talked about Tony but not Bill.

Each felt intense relief—the pain in Bill's stump, compared to what it had been, was easily bearable; his face was almost relaxed. Dojna felt more at ease, more optimistic, than she had felt in years. And yet, at the same time, each felt the most physical presence of the fear that this might not last, that like all their previous hopes this too would fade and disappear. The time felt almost stolen; and if it was. . .they wanted it, still.

It was a strange evening, happy and sad, turning unexpectedly one to the other. Tony had made no decisions; he still lived in limbo. Dr. Kurland's techniques did not hold promise for him; mobility, not relief from pain, was Tony's primary need.

And there was a certain awkwardness Bill and Dojna felt with each other. Adversity had brought them so close; yet, this night, in the midst of their intimacy, there were moments it seemed they had just met. Strange—and wonderful.

That night was an island. Perhaps both of them at some very deep level knew this, even then.

During the next few days Bill's pain grew steadily worse, and soon regained its previous level. But up ahead there was hope. And both Bill and Dojna clung to this.

176

It was summer when Dr. Kurland returned. Bill's treatments began immediately.

At each appointment Dr. Kurland was able to take away Bill's pain—the needles and electronic apparatus were used as in Bill's first appointment. And each time in four or five days the pain returned. Dr. Kurland had originally suggested that this would happen; but the amount of time before the pain returned was supposed to become gradually longer, and the pain was supposed to become less and less intense.

Twenty appointments, one each week, and still the pain returned, as intense as ever. Then it began to return in two or three days, sometimes even one.

Dr. Kurland was baffled. His own instruments had convinced him that Bill's pain was real. His own theories and experience told him the pain should be gone. The acupuncture was working: something had to be short-circuiting its long-term effect. He began, on his own, to do some basic research into prosthetics.

One afternoon he asked to examine Bill's stump; then he asked Bill to demonstrate the use of his prosthesis. Dr. Kurland watched very closely while Bill adjusted the total-contact socket. He watched Bill walk back and forth across the office; and then, asking Bill to stand, he slid a piece of paper under the heel of the prosthesis.

Bill was quite surprised at all this, a passing glance was the most any doctor had ever given his prosthesis. Dr. Kurland had been no exception, up to now.

Bill watched Dr. Kurland examining the limb, his careful attention to key fitting points. It was obvious he was looking for certain things; Dr. Kurland knew something about prosthetics. From a doctor whose interests were presently given to acupuncture, Bill found this doubly surprising. Bill did not, of course, know how recently Dr. Kurland had acquired his knowledge.

Bill waited impatiently for Dr. Kurland to finish. Bill had long before recognized Dr. Kurland as shrewd and genuinely concerned; he wanted to know what Kurland was thinking.

Finally, Dr. Kurland stepped back. He made a disgusted noise. "It doesn't fit!" he said flatly.

Bill waited. It was obvious there was more.

"The heel's not even bearing on the floor," Dr. Kurland continued; "that's got to create a pulling effect on the scar tissue; and I think the socket may be interfering with the circulation of blood. . ." He shook his head, obviously angry. "I'm not a prosthetist; my knowledge here is extremely limited; but that"—he pointed at Bill's prosthesis—"is terrible! You've got to get a decent limb."

"That's what I've said from the beginning," Bill responded.

There was a moment of awkward silence, as Dr. Kurland remembered Bill's story: this was the best of almost a dozen prostheses, from all over the country. Dr. Kurland seemed to be absorbing the implications of this.

Bill made an impatient face and waved the momentary awkwardness away with his hand. He wanted to hear what else Dr. Kurland had to say.

Dr. Kurland continued: "Here's what I think is happening—each week we successfully block the pain, but that contraption you're wearing pulls and bangs away at your stump and reestablishes it. We get diminishing returns from the treatment. Like a black-eye that's being continually battered. The treatment can't keep up. This probably explains your experiences with cortisone shots and lumbar blocks too."

Dr. Kurland shook his head again. "I may be wrong,

178

but I don't think so—you're wasting your time and your money with me, with any doctor; what you need is a leg maker. You need a prosthesis that fits!"

Bill thought back to the first year after the bombing: Dr. Kurland was giving voice to the doubts and suspicions Bill had felt about his prosthetic care, even then. Time and the constant jumble of medical and prosthetic advice had worn this suspicion down, until it was just another strand in the fool's knot he worked to unravel. Now, Dr. Kurland's words brought all those early feelings back to the fore.

"Do you have a prosthetist you can recommend?" Bill asked.

Dr. Kurland went to his desk and retrieved a sheet from Bill's file. "I've collected several names," he said, handing the sheet to Bill, "highly recommended to me. I don't have the knowledge or the exposure to prosthetics to make the judgment myself."

Bill had seen every person named on the list. He was almost in tears: another dead end. But this feeling passed quickly.

Bill was surprised at his own emotions. He found himself not depressed but grim and determined, ready to intensify his search, to find someone who could build a prosthesis. This was step one, it had *always* been step one!

This was a turning point. At this crucial moment, Bill found the strength to take the offensive. He did not understand how, himself.

Perhaps it was the taste of life that Dr. Kurland's treatments had afforded: the days he had spent without pain had given Bill rest, allowed him to hope, and, most important of all, restored his belief that something besides the nightmare he had lived for the past four years could exist. For this Bill was deeply grateful to Dr. Kurland. But there was more, far more. As Bill examined his own emotions, new levels of complexity and insight appeared.

Bill's persistence in trying to see Dr. Kurland had been vindicated. Dr. Kurland had confirmed the reality of Bill's pain. And now Dr. Kurland had confirmed Bill's own earliest convictions about the prosthesis. All this had bolstered Bill's confidence in himself. And still there was more.

Certainly parnaide was playing its role; and the independence and the feelings of competency that had returned with its use. Timing was important: Bill felt that another depression would kill him; he felt, for his very survival, that he must keep the offensive. And it did not escape Bill that this road he was taking led potentially to a solution for Tony, as well as himself. There was almost a sense of relief, as if Bill had known, somewhere within himself all along, that this was the turn events must take.

Bill had gone as far as he could in understanding his own emotions. He felt himself standing firm, perhaps stronger than he had ever been. And he thanked God for this strength, appreciating it fully: for he knew what it was to reach within and find nothing.

It was fall 1974. Bill had renewed his search, this time with a highly specific focus: he was looking for a "leg maker."

He still visited doctors, but only to obtain prosthetic advice and referrals. During these visits he began to press harder and harder for information. He was no longer willing to sit passively and let the doctors prescribe. In the four years since the bombing, Bill had learned a great deal about prosthetics, more, he felt, than was known by all but a handful of the doctors he visited.

Bill's frankness netted a new, and surprising, piece of information. One surgeon confided to Bill: "Mr. Barr, in medical school, prosthetics was covered in just two days of a more general course. I *must* depend on the prosthetist."

Bill was amazed, hardly able to believe what he had heard. But another doctor confirmed the fact and explained: "Prosthetics gets barely a mention in medical school; you see, there are only about a half-million amputees in the whole country, another three million deformed individuals requiring prosthetic care—*very* small numbers."

"Not when you're one of them," Bill had responded.

The discussions of prosthetics widened to surgery. And Bill gleaned new insights.

One doctor told of his internship, amputating limbs in a large city hospital emergency room—knowing he knew nothing of preparing the body for a prosthesis. He had sought guidance but found none. The older surgeons shied away from amputations, leaving it to the less experienced. There was, among doctors, almost a sense of shame, a connotation of failure, that accompanied the word *amputation*; an implicit apology—"I couldn't save the leg." Amputation was the surgery of last resort, relegated to the young surgeons who had no choice. And no one seemed to know much about it. The doctor who told Bill all this had steered his own career away from surgery, as a result of this experience.

Another doctor, amazingly frank, and equally cynical, said the problem was *time*: "There are surgical techniques for amputations," he said, "far better than those in general use—but they take time, and to the surgeon time is money."

And the discussions ranged even wider, with other doctors bemoaning the way the American Medical Association and the media portrayed doctors as "miracle men"—an image they felt no one could live up to. Modern medical technology did seem, in many instances, a miracle, they said, but it wasn't always available; sometimes only a handful of doctors understood or could implement it. And there were numerous areas of medical practice advancing only very slowly. This point struck home with Bill.

He could understand and even empathize with these doctors; as a politician, people had often expected that he too be a man of miracles. And there were politicians, like doctors, who fostered the miracle-man image, just as there were those in both professions who fought against it.

A new perception of doctors, neither black nor white but gray, was forming within Bill. The new information had transformed his thinking: doctors were both better and worse than he had thought. They were human; no less, no more.

Bill had been long in coming to this realization. At first, he had assumed that great knowledge and expertise belonged to every doctor—simply because they were doctors. He too had wanted them to be more than human. There had even been those who had tried to reject this blind faith, but Bill had not been able to hear them, then.

With time, Bill came to hate and fear doctors, all doctors, for not being what he had expected—what the medical publicity men had painted them to be. And he had hated them for the smug complacency and incompetence of a portion of their number. But above all he had hated them for the pain, both physical and emotional, they had caused him and his son.

Now, Bill had come to the center: doctors were people, good and bad—like preachers and plumbers and politicians. This insight was liberating and ironic: it had been frank discussions with doctors about doctors that had freed him of the curse of doctors. Never again would the medical profession have such power to affect his thinking.

Bill continued his search, more convinced than ever that he must find his answers in the field of prosthetics. Here, he ran continuously into what was by now a very familiar brick wall. Prosthetists seemed unable to diagnose the cause of his pain; they were largely unwilling to become involved. Not knowing anything new to try, they deferred back to the doctor: "Diagnoses and prescriptions are *his* responsibility."

Bill felt he had fallen into a crack between doctors and prosthetists; neither knew what to do, and each often blamed the other. The physical therapists he consulted only added to the confusion. It was a replay of his earlier efforts to find help. But now he understood at least something of what he was up against; and this made the difference.

When doctors hinted that his problem was psychological, he ignored them. When prosthetists hinted that he was weak and oversensitive, he knew better. He had confidence in his own perceptions. He was armed with the belief that medical practitioners were mortal. He was determined.

Finally, a medical opinion, which Bill could endorse, began to emerge; it came mostly from doctors and physical therapists, with a very few prosthetists reluctantly nodding yes. One surgeon stated it, succinctly—

"What you need is a total-contact leg that really fits," he said. "I know the theory, but prosthetists are still in the dark ages. I don't know a man who can build one."

"I'm going to find that man," Bill replied, "and I'm going to tell you and the whole goddamn world about him when I do. Bet on it!"

It was two years later, fall 1976, when Bill walked into Dreher Jouett Prosthetics, just north of Chicago. He had, long before, lost track of the number of prosthetists he had visited and the number of prostheses he had had built. He had traveled all over the country.

The last several months Bill had spent pursuing a ghost in the Chicago area: the "old German." Bill had heard stories of an old German, a perfectionist, a genius, who had helped other amputees.

Bill's search had taken him into nearly every prosthetics facility in the area, even into the Chicago ghetto. But no success. Bill guessed the old German was dead, if he had ever really existed in the first place. Then someone had suggested he try Dreher Jouett.

Instead of an old German Bill found Robert, a young man training to be a prosthetist. As he talked with Robert, Bill observed something he had never seen. Robert was fashioning an opaque plastic stump socket; the plaster cast he worked from was covered with blue pencil marks—more marks, by far, than Bill had ever seen on a cast before. Bill began to ask questions.

"New techniques I'm learning from a consultant we're using," answered Robert, "a man named Stokosa."

21

Jan was en route from Lansing to Chicago, on the 8 A.M. commuter flight into O'Hare airport. The difference in time allowed him to land in Chicago at approximately the same clock time he had left Lansing. There was a full day of work ahead.

Once every two weeks Jan made this flight. Robert, from Dreher Jouett Prosthetics, always picked him up at the airport, and by 9 A.M. they would arrive at the Dreher Jouett facility. Robert, ordinarily, had the day carefully planned; he and Jan worked together on fabrication problems in the morning and Jan saw selected patients in the afternoon. But this day was different.

One patient, a millionaire and former legislator who had been car-bombed several years ago, had requested an entire day of Jan's time; and he was willing to pay for it. Jan could not, at the moment, recall the name. But he was glad for the work. His consulting, now three days each week, was subsidizing his own practice and his growing involvement in an amputee ski organization. Both seemed to be in perpetual financial difficulty.

Jan watched out the airplane window. Lake Michigan appeared in glimpses through the clouds, the morning sun starting to glint on the water. No symbolism there, Jan thought to himself: too many bright spots, not enough clouds. He smiled, a bit ruefully, at the joke he had made with himself; and for just a moment wished for someone to share it with. But he was quite used to being alone; his life was his work. It had been so, for almost two years now, ever since he had returned to Michigan. The time had passed so quickly.

And there *are* bright spots, he reminded himself. Another amputee ski clinic was scheduled for the coming winter. Hal O'Leary was coming again from Colorado. The fledgling movement Bill Stieler had started in 1973 had turned into the Central Division Amputee Ski Committee of the United States Ski Association. Jan was totally involved. He was now a fully competent three-track instructor, and gave much of his time to the organization.

Jan had watched several of his patients become deeply involved in skiing. He had watched its dramatic effect on their self-image. These patients, a handful, were the realization of his dream—here was treatment of the *whole* person. But the numbers involved were painfully small, and the ski program teetered constantly on the brink of financial collapse.

Still, Jan told himself, it was a beginning. And it demonstrated what amputees could do, when given the chance.

That was the bright spot. On other fronts, ground had been lost, not gained.

At the Veterans Hospital in Ann Arbor, Michigan, Jan was undergoing a harsh lesson in the politics of change. Here, the past half century of attitudes and practices seemed fully in force: the prosthetist was viewed as a craftsman only, completely subservient to the doctor; and the status of the amputee himself was virtually nonexistent.

And here, the attitudes Jan had found simply unmovable elsewhere had been translated into swift and direct action against him.

For a total of six years, Jan had been a consulting prosthetist at the Ann Arbor Veterans Hospital outpatient amputee clinic; for ten years prior, Walter Stokosa had filled this role. On returning to Michigan, in 1974, Jan had been able to resume this role.

There was a new clinic chief, but the job was much the same. It was Jan who had changed. He was no longer the totally deferential "professional" Walter had trained him to be. He spoke when not spoken to.

He requested more thorough case histories, and time for personal communication with patients, maintaining that until it was known what activities the *amputee* desired to participate in, a prosthesis could not be adequately prescribed. He objected, in private, to the clinic chief, about the way veterans were being used as guinea pigs in the training of students, and not afforded a proper amount of dignity. And finally, in an individual case, he took the side of a veteran, who said he was not being properly fitted.

On June 3, 1975, Jan received a letter from John M. Field, chief of supply service at the Veterans Administration Hospital in Ann Arbor. Underlined, it read: "*A review of the entire situation leaves us with no alternative but to terminate your services for this hospital.*" Veterans were subsequently told by the hospital that Jan's contract to do business with the VA had been canceled.

Jan checked the status of his contract, at the central VA offices. Not only was it still in force, but the VA commented that in sixteen years of service, neither Stokosa had a single mark against his name. They would look into the problem.

The VA Hospital in Allen Park, Michigan, continued to give Jan referrals. Some long-time Stokosa patients switched from the Ann Arbor facility to the one in Allen Park. Others decided to fight.

One veteran wrote to his congressman: "I have lost a

187

leg for my country—I can accept this. I have lost my prosthetist to bureaucratic red tape—I don't have to accept this." Another veteran, who before seeing Jan had been in a great deal of pain, offered to "mail in my purple heart." Other letters were similar.

Finally, the VA sent out an investigator, a Mr. Anthony Staros. From his report:

> Indeed the work of all the prosthetic laboratories observed was found to be excellent. And this observation includes the work of Prosthetic Services of Lansing (sole proprietor Jan J. Stokosa) which we felt, in the one case observed, was perhaps of the highest quality we have observed anywhere.

And later in the same report:

> He [Jan] has demonstrated excellent workmanship and apparently some skills in dealing with patients since some do prefer to go to him for reasons other than geography.

And finally:

> We cannot now support any consideration for cancellation [of Jan's VA contract], especially since VAH Allen Park thinks highly of his [Jan's] services.

This had been almost a year ago. And despite the official vindication, Jan was still refused entry to the Ann Arbor VA Hospital; and veterans were still being told they could not come to him.

Jan was learning that being right is far less than halfway to winning a battle. And the Ann Arbor VA, albeit the worst, was still only one of the many brick walls Jan had

188

run into. The prosthetics establishment—the chains, the professional associations, the national VA, the insurance companies, and many doctors—seemed to like things just the way they were. Jan met individual amputees and individual prosthetists who, like himself, saw the need for, and advocated, change. But he was coming to realize that people like himself were very small fish, swimming against a very large current.

For now, there was only individual success: Jan's own patients were being optimally fitted, many of them returning to activities thought impossible for amputees, some learning to ski; and the consulting work, with its steady diet of problem cases, was a constant challenge. Jan felt his skill as a prosthetist was growing. But the obstacles to widespread change in the field of prosthetics seemed unmovable. The goals Jan had for his profession appeared a long way off, perhaps unreachable.

Through the airplane window, Chicago came into view. Jan put aside his thoughts, ready, even anxious, to lose himself in the intricacies of an individual case. *William G. Barr*, he remembered the name, as the plane touched down.

Bill was at Dreher Jouett when Jan arrived. His first impression was that Jan was too young; he had expected someone much older: an image of an old man in a white coat had unconsciously materialized in Bill's mind. Jan wore a leather vest with bright nickel buttons.

Robert made the introductions, and Jan immediately began his examination of Bill's X-rays and stump, and Bill's existing prosthesis. As Jan did this, Bill gave him the history.

Jan listened in silence, his face revealing nothing. He seemed to ask any questions he had with his hands, alternately handling Bill's stump and prosthesis as Bill talked. Bill had become very adept at reading the non-verbal clues which indicated doubt or uncertainty—he watched Jan very closely.

Jan's total silence was unusual, but Bill quickly recognized it as concentration. The fact that Jan had made no attempt to sell himself, had, in fact, said nothing about himself at all, spelled competence to Bill. And there was no doubt that Jan believed him, accepted the reality of his pain.

Bill found himself with the comforting feeling that, already, Jan was totally involved and on his side. But Bill guarded his feelings; others had looked good at this point too.

Jan had Bill put on his old prosthesis and walk back and forth, in the examining room. Jan lay on the floor to watch Bill walk; he identified a number of bad habits Bill had literally built into his gait. After suggesting several corrective measures for Bill to try, Jan suddenly stood up. "Time for this later," he said.

Robert had already made a test socket of Bill's stump, an opaque plastic socket that could be attached with a pylon to a temporary knee and foot. Bill was fitted with this temporary leg and taken to a set of parallel bars.

Again, Jan lay on the floor while Bill walked. Minor adjustments were made in the temporary knee. And then, after more walking, the test socket was removed. Jan disappeared into another room, returning with the test socket drilled full of holes. It was refitted and Jan tested the tension of the skin on Bill's stump by inserting a bamboo rod through the holes.

Bill was fascinated. All this was totally new to him. He had the distinct impression he was watching an artist at work. And, still, Jan had said virtually nothing.

Bill could contain himself no longer. He began to ask questions. The test socket—which had caught his attention in the first place and caused him to learn of Stokosa—"where did it come from, what did it do?"

Robert was enthusiastic about the procedure, explaining that Jan had learned it from his father and then had added some ideas of his own. "Except in rare cases," Robert said, "building a prosthesis without a test socket is like choosing a pair of shoes without ever having stood up or taken a step in them."

Bill had the feeling he was hearing Jan's words, through Robert.

"Does anyone else do test sockets?" Bill asked. He aimed the question directly at Jan.

"Of course," Jan said; "I'm sure many prosthetists use them.

Robert looked skeptical.

"Then why haven't *I* ever seen one before?" Bill asked.

Jan did not answer, deliberately focusing his attention back on his work. Bill felt strong forces operating within Jan; he sensed that Jan wanted to talk about this but would not. But Bill wanted an answer.

"You can talk to *me*," he said, "I'm practically an honorary prosthetist. I've had a dozen legs made, you know."

Still, Jan said nothing but continued to evaluate the test socket, moving Bill's stump back and forth and feeling the effect with the bamboo rod.

"All right," Bill said, speaking almost to himself, "we can talk about this later." Bill was beginning to sense just how unusual and highly complex Jan Stokosa was.

Jan was making a similar observation about Bill.

22

An hour passed, then two. Jan had rejected the initial test socket and was studying Bill's stump to build a second. He reexamined the stump itself, and the X-rays. He had Bill walk back and forth between the parallel bars, on both Bill's old prosthesis and on the new, temporary limb. Jan watched from every conceivable angle. There was more probing with the bamboo rod. And then this process would start all over.

The cause of Bill's pain was coming together, like a puzzle, in Jan's mind. He sensed very early that there was no single cause, but several, at the root of the problem. He kept his own counsel and continued the examination. Slowly he sorted it out.

Bill's stump was badly bruised from a generally poorly fitted and poorly aligned prosthesis. Bill exacerbated this by the way he walked. But these were only compounding factors.

There were, as Jan saw it, two major problems. First, in Bill's prosthesis there was a finger-width space between the bottom of the stump socket and the end of Bill's stump. This space was more than enough to create "negative pressure" and interfere with the return circulation of blood—a situation similar in effect to placing a rubber band near the end of a finger.

The second major problem was a muscle in Bill's thigh; Jan noted that with each step one of the quadriceps was being pulled into an unnatural position. Jan guessed that the muscle had become detached in the bombing and had readhered out of its normal position. This situation would become a problem *only* in combination with a prosthesis. Jan was sure that many of the surgeons who had examined Bill had noted this malaligned muscle but had not grasped its prosthetic implications.

Another test socket was needed, the one Robert had made was quite good but it did not take the unusual thigh muscle into account. A stump socket designed to allow for this muscle would help—but, even with the best of sockets, revision surgery might still be necessary.

By the time Jan had organized these thoughts it was past noon. Over lunch, he explained his thinking to Bill.

"Where does that leave us?" Bill asked, when Jan had finished.

"First, the new test socket," Jan had said. "Then a whole new prosthesis; I think we can make a number of basic improvements. That will be step one."

Jan continued: "Your stump will stabilize its size and shape, and heal; right now, it is badly swollen. When this happens, we'll have to build a second socket, perhaps even a third. And then there's still the chance you'll have to have the revision surgery anyway." Jan paused. "I know that must sound like a long road to go, but you've been misusing your stump for over six years; it's going to take time to reverse that. And it's the only way to do it *right*," he added.

Bill nodded. He had watched Jan work for several hours now; and he had made up his mind. "Then that's what we'll do," he said; "the question is how soon can we do it."

Bill settled up with Dreher Jouett and arranged to see Jan in Lansing. He was not content to wait until Jan's next visit to Chicago.

Bill had a strong gut feeling that this was his man.

He offered to pay Jan double for the initial prosthesis, if Jan would begin right away. Jan refused; there were other patients already scheduled.

"What would it take?" Bill asked.

"It's not for sale," Jan said, a warning tone in his voice.

Bill sensed immediately that this was the wrong tack, and pulled himself back. At the same time Jan was feeling Bill's need. After six years of pain, who would not be trying to make things happen more quickly? Jan regretted his curt reply.

"All right," he recanted, "I'll fit you in. But we may be working in the middle of the night—and the price doesn't change."

Bill put his hands out, palms down, calming the waters. "All right," Bill said, "you'll get no arguments from me. . .but I'll tell you what: I offered the extra money, how about if I give it to a good cause, of your choice?"

Jan smiled and nodded. He understood pride. Bill was a man, in ways, not unlike himself. And Jan was thinking of the ski program.

"I'm involved in an amputee ski program," Jan said. "It could certainly use the money."

Bill knew he had struck a nerve. "How much trouble is the program in?" he asked.

"About five thousand dollars' worth," Jan said.

Bill smiled. "You build me this leg in one week, starting now, and I'll give your ski program the five thousand and still pay you for the leg."

Jan looked directly at Bill's eyes. "All right," he said, "only you *don't* pay me for the leg."

Bill smiled broadly. "Done," he said. Jan offered his hand. And Bill took it.

The next day, a Wednesday, Bill was on the 8 A.M. commuter flight from Chicago to Lansing. A taxi was waiting when he arrived. He made one stop to check into a hotel and then went directly to Jan's place of business.

A small sign, "Prosthetic Services," stood outside an old house on a downtown street. Upstairs the house was converted into casting and fitting rooms, and a large open space with parallel bars and a full-length mirror; downstairs it had been turned into a workshop. There was a patchwork look to the place, but it was sturdy and clean.

Jan had managed to reschedule one of his weekly consulting visits; and another he had been able to cut to half a day. The rest of the time needed to fabricate and fit Bill's leg would be stolen between regular patients, and at night, plus the weekend.

Jan immediately took a new plaster cast of Bill's stump, marking it with a blue pencil; the outside of the cast began to look like a map of an intricate river system.

Jan explained as he worked: the nerves and muscles and prominent bones—especially the unusually placed thigh muscle—all must be allowed for in the socket, which was built from the cast.

Bill had had his stump cast perhaps fifteen or twenty times before. It usually took only minutes. Jan spent well over an hour. Next the test socket was made and tried out on a temporary leg. Several more hours had passed. Jan was not satisfied with the results and began the procedure all over.

On crutches, Bill followed Jan up and down the stairs, watching him work, and talking. Always talking. Bill was full of questions, and stories about his past experiences with doctors and prosthetists.

Jan sensed that this was Bill's way of diverting himself from the pain. But there was more than that: it was clear that Bill was piecing together a very critical picture of prosthetic care in the United States; an accurate picture, Jan judged.

Still, Jan was not ready to talk about this to an outsider. He confirmed Bill's observations about the lack of prosthetic knowledge on the part of doctors in general, he acknowledged that the prosthesis Bill had been wearing was improperly fitted—but he was not willing to talk freely, to contribute to this discussion, not yet. Too many years of living Walter's conception of the professional stood in his way.

Jan felt great anxiety in the presence of Bill's questions. Jerry Turner, the young Vietnam veteran Jan had encountered while he worked at the prosthetics shop in Jacksonville, came often to his mind. Since that time Jan had become a vocal proponent of change in the prosthetics profession but only *within* the profession had he spoken. His recent difficulties with the VA were the closest he had come to voicing public criticism. And he had paid dearly for that.

Now, Bill Barr was almost badgering him to come out in the open, to give full voice to his feelings—*to a patient*. And something about Bill told Jan that it would not end there. Bill had suffered for over six years, but unlike most people he wanted more than relief. Jan sensed that Bill wanted to understand the suffering, and planned to *do something* about it. Jan felt Bill's oath. It had no cognitive shape in Jan's mind; it was Bill's determination, focused beyond the self, that Jan felt—and saw in Bill's eyes. Jan had seen this same look in Walter's eyes, many times.

This frightened Jan. Bill had already had several pieces of the puzzle in place—the same jigsaw image of prosthetic care that Jan himself had been piecing together. Bill had several of the pieces, but not all. How would Bill respond? What would he do?

Almost as a reflex, Jan felt protective of his profession. It was obvious that Bill was, both by force of his personality and by his wealth, a powerful man. *What would he do?*

At the same time, Jan felt a strong bond with Bill. Were they not natural allies? And on a personal level Jan respected Bill, his straightforwardness and obvious intelligence. And Jan marveled at the way Bill managed his pain.

Jan grappled with his feelings, all this first day. It was almost midnight when they stopped work. Bill and Jan had spent almost fifteen hours together.

Before they left for the night, Jan asked Bill to wrap his stump, pointing to a cabinet where elastic bandages were kept. Jan was cleaning and putting away tools. Bill fumbled with a bandage, achieving a loose-fitting, unstable wrap.

Jan showed Bill how to join two bandages together and secure the wrap, alpine-climber-style, around his waist. It was totally secure.

"Now why has no one else ever showed me that?" Bill asked. It was a pointed question. A dozen times, this day, Bill had asked the same question in other ways.

But Jan was not ready to answer.

The next day, Thursday, Jan had to be in Detroit. Bill spent the day impatiently waiting in his hotel.

Friday and Saturday, Jan and Bill worked nonstop. Gradually Bill began to gain Jan's confidence. Bill stayed with Jan in the workshop, past midnight each night. For meals, they ate hamburgers together, from a nearby drive-in. And they talked.

The wall around Jan, very gradually, began to come down. Jan talked, guardedly, about his past; about the rigorous training he had received as a boy; about Walter. Bill told Jan about Tony, the frustration he felt at not being able to help. Bill and Jan were becoming friends.

On Sunday, Bill took his first steps on the new prosthesis. It was not cosmetically finished, but the basic elements were in place. It had a plastic, total-contact socket and a light hydraulic knee, and the ankle had a rotator that allowed the foot lateral motion. There was a button that, when pushed, locked the leg stiffly in place, for long periods of standing. Another button released it completely. Bill had seen nothing like it.

But walking told the real story.

"It's light," Bill said, after a trip up and back between the parallel bars.

"No, it fits," Jan said. "It actually weighs a little more than your old one."

Bill continued to walk. Up and back, several more times, and his stump started to feel warm—a measure of his pain began to subside. An incredible excitement was building within him: *this was going to work; it was going to work!*

In Bill's face, Jan read what was happening. "Circulation," he said, simply; and smiled.

Bill walked in silence, concentrating deeply, for another fifteen minutes; his excitement grew as he got the feel of his new prosthesis. Jan had to ask him, twice, to sit down.

"It's fantastic!" Bill said. "On certain steps I swear I could *feel* my foot." Bill was breathing hard, not from exertion but from the excitement. His pain was not gone but the reduction had been dramatic—and it was going to get better; he knew it. "I felt my foot!" he repeated.

"It's called proprioception," Jan said, "a phantom sensation, like a phantom pain, only positive. I think you'll be feeling more of that." Jan realized that Bill had stopped listening.

Bill found himself filled with nervous energy, his mind racing ahead to the stabilization and complete healing of his stump, to Jan helping Tony.

"Look, Stokosa, don't just stand there," he said. "You just fixed my damned leg—ask me to dance, kiss me; something. . ."

That night, from his hotel, Bill called Tony. Jan had cautioned Bill that there was a long way to go in Bill's case, and that there was no certainty that Tony could be helped at all. But Bill had walked on a *Stokosa leg*, he had watched Jan work for four long days. He was sure he was on the right track.

Tony listened but was unmoved; he had made an adjustment to his situation, he was getting by. "I'm not getting back on that merry-go-round," he told Bill, "no more doctors, no more prosthetists—not again." And Bill could not budge him.

Bill stayed in Lansing two and a half days more. Jan worked on the cosmetic aspects of the prosthesis and made some final adjustments, and gave Bill walking lessons several hours each day. The walking seemed actually to lessen his pain—"increased circulation," as Jan had explained. Bill was successfully wrapping his stump overnight, and was continuing to feel a good measure of relief. He was totally optimistic. And more determined than ever for Jan to answer his questions.

It was Jan, however, who finally opened the discussion Bill had been wanting. They sat in the workshop, eating pizza for breakfast, left over from the night before.

"You know, Stokosa," Bill said, "you are without a doubt the finest prosthetist in the country, but the food here is *terrible!*"

Both of them were very tired and they laughed a long time, stopping and starting up again, several times. Jan liked Bill a great deal. And he had been thinking a lot about Bill's questions. Didn't six years of pain entitle someone to an answer?

"Bill," Jan said, when they had finally stopped laughing, "I'd like to answer your questions, as I see things."

Both men became suddenly serious. For the next several hours they sat and discussed prosthetics: training, certification, the chains, doctors and their lack of prosthetic knowledge, and what all this meant to amputees. Much of what they discussed came as a bombshell to Bill. After all these years, he still labored under the misconception that prosthetists were doctors of some sort. "Eighteen weeks of training," he repeated in disbelief; "no licensing!"

For the first time, Bill began fully to understand the nightmare he had lived since the bombing: the complete *reason* why he had not been able to find help was taking shape. Simultaneously, a new mystery presented itself—Stokosa.

"I'd like to talk to some of your patients," Bill said suddenly. "Can you give me some names and phone numbers?"

Jan simply stared, his mind drawing blank, but his feelings were telling him that *something* was starting. Hadn't he told himself that if he talked to Bill, *it wouldn't end there.*

"I promise not to say bad things about you," Bill said.

Jan nodded and smiled. He could not sort out his feelings. But at the bottom line, he knew that Bill Barr had become his friend. Jan trusted him. "All right," he said.

On Wednesday morning, the agreed-upon day, Bill's leg was finished. Bill handed Jan the check for the ski association. "I can't start to tell you. . . ," Bill began. Jan held up his hand.

"We've a long way to go," he said. "And it's mine to thank you." Jan held up the check. "Some of your brother and sister amputees will be skiing this winter."

"I'll call you about an appointment for my son," Bill said.

Jan nodded. They shook hands and Bill went to a waiting taxi. The plane reservation he had waiting was not for Chicago, but for Florida.

23

It was November when a meeting was finally arranged. Jan arrived in Joliet on a Friday evening and was with Bill and Dojna, waiting. All three drove together to Chicago's O'Hare airport on a Saturday morning to meet Tony. No one had voiced it but there was a great fear that he would not show.

A month had passed since Bill had visited Tony in Florida. Tony had remained skeptical of the possibility that Jan could help him. And whether or not Tony would come to see Jan remained the question.

Tony had become numb to his own situation, evolving a lifestyle that put him on his feet as little as possible. He conducted his real estate business, insofar as possible, from behind his desk or from a car. And he had almost learned not to think about the athletic activities that had once been so central to his life.

Bill saw this not as adjustment but as avoidance. Tony was not facing his handicap, he was denying life. Bill felt Tony drifting into a private world, where just getting by was the aim and striving did not exist. This was anathema to Bill Barr. Soon, Bill thought, Tony would be lost, even to himself.

Bill wanted desperately to rush in and, with the strength of his own personality, force Tony to come with him, to make Tony try. Bill had done this in the past, he knew. He had brought Tony to Chicago to have a prosthesis built, in a desperate attempt to help, nearly three years before. The impression had lasted. Tony had come only to please Bill. Even if the trip had been successful, it would have been Bill's victory, not Tony's. And, as it turned out, it was Bill's failure.

Bill would not make this mistake again. If Tony's spirit was sacrificed to make his body whole, what would be gained? Bill was emerging from his own ordeal, with his spirit intact; he was in a unique position to assess the value of this—and, to him, the value was ultimate. He could not rob his own son of the chance to do the same.

Tony must be strong for himself; no one could do it for him. This thought was clear, yet all Bill's emotions pulled him away from what he knew he must do.

Bill thought of Dojna, standing beside him, supporting him, all those six years since the bombing, but never had she done anything that took away his dignity. She never had been strong for him but had helped him, and let him be strong himself. Within, Bill thanked her anew, and with deep understanding. And it was these thoughts of Dojna, now, that helped him again to be strong.

Bill spoke plainly to Tony: "I think Stokosa can help you," he said. "I'll set up a meeting. But don't come for me, I won't put that on you. Tony, if you can't come for yourself, don't come at all."

Of everything Bill had gone through, this was perhaps the hardest.

Tony recognized Chicago below, as the airplane made its landing approach. He was not glad to be here. He did not really believe anything would be changed by this visit.

But he *was* coming of his own volition. His father's words had struck home. They had made him angry, first at Bill, then at himself; and then at doctors and prosthetists, all over again. Tony's comforting cocoon of inaction was broken, and the turmoil of his emotions had been loosed. He did not believe, but he had started once more to hope.

The relief, in Dojna and Bill, at seeing Tony emerge from the airline gate quickly gave way to a larger anxiety: would Jan be able to help him? Jan's outward appearance gave no hint of a first reaction, but Bill sensed that Jan was already at work, studying Tony's walk.

Tony's knee wobbled badly, as he awkwardly hop walked toward them. Pain was visible in his face, beneath a studied mask of indifference. He did not make eye contact with anyone.

Bill and Dojna greeted him, an emotional greeting, spending some of the pent-up anxiety that all of them were feeling. Tony and Jan were introduced, and the four of them went to retrieve Tony's luggage and return to Joliet.

Over lunch, in the Black Road apartment, Jan heard Tony's story. Bill had already briefed Jan, but there were many details that Jan wanted from Tony himself.

Tony told his story, dispassionately, under great self-control. He had brought with him, in a shopping bag, the half-dozen prostheses that had been built for him, and he handed them to Jan at the appropriate place in his narrative. Jan made no comment, as he examined each one, but he could not prevent a flicker of dismay from crossing his face.

Tony ended his story by crumpling a sheet of newspaper into a ball. He tossed it to Jan.

"Here," Tony said, "I forgot to bring my very first prosthesis. Put that with the others—make the set complete!" Tony's anger and frustration flashed for only this instant. He quickly regained his self-control.

Jan knew the outburst had been aimed, at least in part,

at him—disappointment, in advance: Tony did not dare believe he was finally going to be helped. Jan did not blame him. It was far from the first time Jan had absorbed such emotion from a patient; he let it roll off him and asked Tony if he had been able to bring X-rays. Tony rummaged inside a briefcase and handed a large envelope to Jan.

For the next twenty minutes Jan seemed to forget the people around him. He studied one X-ray and then another, going back to the first, a side view of Tony's stump, several times. The others sipped coffee and waited.

"Shall we have a look?" Jan finally said.

Tony pulled up his pantleg and Jan, dropping to one knee, removed Tony's shoe and sock. The stump was oozing slightly; Dojna went immediately for warm water and cloths. She and Jan bathed the wound and placed Tony's foot on a towel. Bill smoked cigarettes, one after the other. Tony stared off into space; he seemed almost bored.

The problem was apparent. Jan was far from the first to diagnose it. The angle of Tony's stump was downward, making a balanced step impossible. Jan had known this from the X-rays alone. Prosthetically, the problem was to lift the stump and create a flat step, without introducing a lateral wobble at the ankle or knee. It would be very tricky. There was a great deal to consider. Jan had had only one similar case in his entire career, and the angle had been nowhere nearly as extreme.

"You're absolutely opposed to the revision surgery?" Jan asked.

Tony nodded.

Jan went back to examining the stump, frequently holding one of the X-rays up to the light and studying it.

Another twenty minutes went by. Tony had begun to

drum on the table with his fingers. In the ashtray beside Bill, the remains of a half-dozen cigarettes were crumpled. Only Dojna had remained quiet, her concentration almost one with Jan's.

"I think it can be done," Jan finally said, speaking directly to Tony. "But no promises. I've never done what I have in mind before."

Tony was silent for a long moment. The merry-go-round he wanted so desperately to be off seemed to be starting up all over again. He found himself almost believing, God help him, once more. He looked to Dojna and his father. They understood, he knew. They said nothing, and he understood that.

Tony nodded. It was done.

That evening Tony and Jan left on a plane for Lansing, to make the attempt, to try.

As Jan and Tony disappeared down the corridor to their Lansing flight, Bill's thoughts turned back to himself. His stump was visibly healing; the discoloration, which had been present almost from the start, was gone. His pain was manageable and steadily declining. Of all of the treatments he had undergone, some of which had shown promise initially, this was the first in which a pattern of steady improvement had been established.

Bill was looking ahead. As his own condition improved, he gave more and more time to analyzing the ordeal he had come through—and thinking of others still, and yet to be, trapped in a similar nightmare. He had made a vow, and he was all but sure that he had found the means of fulfilling it.

During the last month Bill had talked, both by telephone and in person, with a large number of Jan's patients. Bill wanted to confirm, beyond any doubt, that Jan was the genius he thought him to be. The patient list Jan had supplied Bill with was in alphabetical order. The very first name on the list gave Bill what he was looking for.

Gaylord Acker had lost his arm in an industrial accident in 1953. He had had five different prostheses, all with encumbering straps, and he had lived with considerable pain. The best of these prostheses he had been able to wear only a few hours per day. Then he met Jan.

Jan fitted him with a strapless arm, complete with a realistic-looking functional hand. The hand was myoelectrically powered—controlled by thought impulses from the brain, picked up through the muscles of the upper arm.

Acker had heard of the existence of this "bionic" arm before, but he had been consistently advised against it, both by doctors and by prosthetists. He was told that it was "temperamental" and "unreliable." He was deeply grateful to Jan for proving this advice wrong.

Gaylord Acker was a schoolteacher. With his new myoelectric prosthesis, he could write with chalk on the blackboard; and, with a pen, he could record grades in the tiny columns of a classbook. He was free of confining straps, and wore his new prosthesis twelve hours each day, without pain.

Bill had been looking for verification of his opinion of Jan. But this was a far more dramatic beginning than even he had expected. It continued.

Howard Bush was seventy-four years old; both his legs were gone, below the knee. He had had nine pairs of artificial limbs, with straps that, in his own words, "kept me so hunched over I couldn't do anything." He spent the better part of five years in a chair, able to wear his prostheses for only very brief periods of time. But he wanted to walk, to work, to return to a more normal life. And he would not give up. Then he met Jan.

On strapless Stokosa legs, Howard Bush was able to climb a ladder, to carry his fifty-pound toolbox, to pick up a dime off the floor.

A full-page feature article, recounting these accomplishments, was done on Howard Bush in his hometown paper, the *Jackson* (Michigan) *Citizen Patriot*. A local prosthetist called Bush the day the article appeared. "Why do you let them print all those lies about you?" the prosthetist asked. Howard Bush invited the prosthetist to come to his home to see for himself. The prosthetist never showed.

Bill continued to call and to visit Stokosa patients. He met *Connie Gardner*, a black woman weighing 250 pounds. Both of her legs had been amputated below the knee. Doctors and physical therapists had told her she would never walk. But she did. She even climbed stairs. Her admiration for Jan was boundless.

Bill shared a bond with these people. He loved them for their courage. He had known their suffering. They were his brothers and sisters. He became even more determined to fulfill the oath he had taken, to *do something* about the plight of amputees—all amputees.

The list of Stokosa patients was long. There were many dramatic stories, but certainly not every case. Bill talked to a great many simply satisfied patients. He often asked such patients how they had come to *find* Jan. One person replied: "I looked up prosthetics in the phone book." Bill did not know whether to laugh or cry.

At the end of his inquiries, one case stood out in Bill's mind. *Lon Sandborn*, sixteen years old, had lost part of his foot in a lawnmower accident. Like Tony, Lon had been fitted with numerous prostheses but remained severely crippled.

Now, wearing a Stokosa limb, Lon was able to run. He had even resumed playing football and baseball at school.

What would Jan be able to do for Tony? Jan had cautioned Bill not to set his hopes too high. Tony's was the worst case of its type Jan had ever seen.

Jan had promised to call Bill as soon as he knew anything. It was over a week before the call came.

Tony climbed onto a chair for the third time in a row. "What if I break it?" he asked.

"Go ahead," Jan answered, "but I doubt you can."

"I can skydive, then, no problem?"

"You can do anything you can do," Jan answered.

Tony gave out a war whoop and leaped to the floor. Without pause he ran up the stairs from Jan's workshop and out the back door of the building.

Jan followed and found Tony running windsprints in the parking lot. He watched for a time, pleased with the full stride Tony was taking. "Hey, be careful," Jan shouted, "you're not in condition, you'll hurt your lungs." Jan smiled. It had been a long week.

He and Tony had worked together, much as he and Bill had done. Except Tony had been very quiet, until now.

There were some cosmetic touches to be finished on Tony's prosthesis but basically it was completed: a light plastic shell that encased Tony's foot and leg to just below the knee, lifting his stump and creating a virtually normal step. A regular shoe, of Tony's normal size, could be worn over it. The difficulty had been all the interrelated angles, of knee and ankle and the downward-tilting stump, horizontal and vertical forces—more a problem of physics than of anything else, Jan thought. And somewhere, deep within himself, he thanked Walter for all the hard lessons in the mathematics of anatomy.

Three times, before striking upon the final design, Jan scrapped a nearly completed prosthesis; and each time, within himself, Jan questioned the feasibility of the project.

Each time, as they started over, Jan felt Tony wanting to quit. But Tony kept on, working *with* Jan, not just passively staying until it was over. Jan appreciated this and admired Tony for it.

And Tony felt the effort that Jan was expending. As they started again, for the fourth time, Tony thanked Jan "either way."

Now, Tony was in the parking lot running, and Jan felt very good. Jan came back inside and called Bill.

"I think I can say we've been successful," Jan said.

"What does that mean?" Bill almost shouted.

Jan's voice remained calm. "It means that Tony has regained significant mobility and. . ."

Bill interrupted. "Where's Tony?"

"Out running in the parking lot," Jan said.

"Running!" Bill yelled into the phone. "Stokosa, you make me so damned mad—but I love ya. Get me Tony."

"Right away," Jan said. He was smiling.

24

It was the new year, 1977. And for Tony Barr a new life had begun. Tony's recovery was far beyond any hopes he had dared. Jan had greatly helped Bill; for Tony he had performed a small miracle.

Tony was, once again, skydiving each weekend. He could land on two feet with no pain. He could run as fast as ever and could even play tennis. He was leading a normal life, meeting people, dating. In retrospect, Tony realized how isolated he had become. He felt awakened from a nightmare, a nightmare that had lasted four years.

It was as if there were three different people: one who had lived the twenty-odd years before his accident, another for the past four years. And now he was a third person, discovering himself anew each day.

He felt, in time, the three views of himself would merge. There were strong threads connecting them even now. Tony felt the importance of this, and he wondered how he would ultimately have viewed himself if the decision to see Jan had not been his own; he sensed that this was a critical thread, that might have been broken, just as it might have if he had not rallied himself a dozen other times during his ordeal. He was grateful to his father for helping him see this, for helping him find himself once more. And, of course, he was grateful to Bill for finding Jan.

Often, now, Tony thought of that very first day on his new prosthesis, and of his reunion with Bill. He had taken the morning flight straight from Lansing to Chicago.

He walked from the plane, through the flight gate to the main terminal, confident in his step, noticing that no one was noticing *him at all.* As he passed the rows of newspaper-disp   nes, he remembered clearly the day, a lifet   when he had walked this way, passing the   at told in bold print of the bombing and of h   r death.

And then   ddenly jarred back to the present. His fathers' arms were around him and both were crying.

Even now, almost two months later, Tony still cried as he remembered this meeting.

The new year. And a new life had begun for Bill too, in part because a new life had begun for his son, but only in part.

Bill's pain was no longer the central focus of his life; it had decreased to the point where a normal existence was possible. He and Dojna were planning a new house. They had taken a Christmas vacation in Florida. Bill was becoming reacquainted with his children and his friends. The years since 1970 were blurring together, behind him.

The bombing remained an unsolved crime. Several suspects had been apprehended and then released for lack of evidence. The investigation had slowly come to a standstill. Who ordered the bombing was now only a topic of cocktail-party speculation. The case was officially open, but that was all. Bill guessed the bombing would always remain unsolved. This held no anguish for him. It was past.

The mystery that did concern Bill was why it had taken six years for him to find help. Why six years until he had finally been fitted with an adequate prosthesis? Why had Tony needlessly suffered for so long? Why the stories he had now heard from so many other amputees?

Bill felt he had this mystery largely unraveled, he had the various strands well in hand; their interest to him lay not in the past tense but only in the future. Understanding what had happened was only the necessary first step in doing something about it.

Bill sat across from Jan in a posh Lansing restaurant. Jan sipped a glass of wine; a cup of coffee sat before Bill. It was February 1977.

They had just completed work on Bill's second prosthesis. Bill felt very good; he had walked more than a mile this day, and his leg felt better than ever. But this had nothing to do with what he was saying. He had been planning this conversation, very carefully, for a long time.

"Here are the two prongs of the problem," he said, sliding silver salt and pepper shakers into position, alongside each other in front of him—"the doctor and the prosthetist. The doctor," Bill touched one of the shakers, "the surgeon in particular, isn't using prosthetically oriented amputation procedures. Most surgeons don't even know about them, some won't take the time—a variety of reasons. But the bottom line is, they're just chopping off legs and arms, not preparing the body for a prosthesis. On top of this, it's the doctor, lacking the most basic knowledge of prosthetics, who prescribes the prosthesis itself. Incredible! At the root of this *doctor* problem, we've got a number of things: lack of preparation in medical schools, lack of communication with prosthetists, the AMA's miracle-man image...a number of things." Bill paused.

"Now let's look at the prosthetist," he tapped the other silver shaker. "Here we've got a widespread lack of skill—a performance problem. And along with this, actually a part of this, there is a tremendous underutilization of available technology. Stone-age stuff—you wouldn't *believe* some of the work I've seen!" Bill stopped. He smiled. "Yeah, well, I guess you've seen it too. I get a little carried away."

Jan smiled. He too had gotten carried away at times, making this same point.

"Anyway," Bill resumed, tapping the shaker again, "behind this *prosthetist* problem, we've got the prosthetic associations and the major prosthetic chains holding hands and controlling the industry: self-regulation. We've got a laughable education and training program for prosthetists; and we've got a standard of pay, and accompanying status, that can in no way attract talented people to the profession." Bill was not quite finished. He reached across to another table, picked up another silver shaker, and placed it between the first two.

"The physical therapist," he said, tapping the new shaker, "caught in the middle. How can he possibly do his job until the doctor and the prosthetist do theirs. Hell, nobody even knows what to tell him to do. He's a blind man, trying to spin gold out of straw."

Jan sat staring at the three silver shakers. Bill had just stated Jan's own position, only more clearly and in a more organized manner than Jan had ever stated it himself. Jan was beginning to understand what made Bill Barr a millionaire and a master politician.

"Now, here's the rub," Bill said.

Jan settled back; he was anxious to listen.

"If the problem is approached like this," Bill motioned to the horizontal row of shakers before him, "everything gets confused. We end up with a big pissing match over details and who's to blame. Listen to this." Bill pulled a briefcase onto the table and took out a stack of papers; he sorted out several.

214

"From one of your own prosthetic journals," he said, "a surgeon is talking about an advance in amputation surgery." Bill read: " '*It seems to be impossible to get a limbmaker to get out of his groove and make a suitable limb for such a stump.*' " Bill looked up. "You know when that was written? 1923."

Bill shook his head. "I've got articles here taking the other side—that prosthetists can't get surgeons to do the correct surgery. And physical therapists, frustrated with everybody. It gets nowhere! A big pissing match, that's all. I've seen it in politics a thousand times. If the problem is approached like this," Bill motioned again to the row of silver shakers, "we get lost responding to symptoms, we never get to the roots of the problem."

Jan stared at the stack of medical and prosthetic journal articles, piled beside the three silver shakers. Bill had now gone beyond clarifying Jan's thoughts; Bill was breaking new ground in *understanding* the problem.

"Okay," Jan said. "What do we do about it?"

Bill smiled. "I was hoping you'd ask," he said.

25

Bill rearranged the shakers, from their horizontal row, into a line between himself and Jan. He touched the shaker nearest him, "the prosthetist," he said, and then the next two in order, "the physical therapist; the doctor." Bill tapped on the table directly in front of the prosthetist shaker. "Right here is where we attack the problem," he said, "and align the whole thing—third-party licensing and control."

It was late. Bill and Jan had been talking for several hours. The silver shakers still formed a line between them. They had just sent the waiter away for what seemed like the nineteenth time: they were not yet ready to order.

Bill was arguing for a stringent test, to be conducted by an interested third party, probably the individual states. The state would then issue a license to practice, just as in medicine and law. This had been an integral part of what Jan had been advocating for prosthetics for the past two years.

In his mind, Jan traced the lines Bill had verbally drawn, from the licensing of prosthetists back to the problems that had been earlier stated. In prosthetics, licensing would automatically loosen association/chain control of the profession, breaking down the assembly-line, high-profit-margin mentality; more advanced technology and procedures would have a chance to compete, and insurance companies, the VA, and other government agencies would have to face the reality of higher prices; licensing, backed by a stringent test, would force educational institutions to expand their programs and train more diligently in order that their students might be able to enter the field. These things, in turn, would raise the status and pay of prosthetists and attract more talented people to the profession. All of which struck at the heart of the problem—inadequate prosthetic care.

And Bill had not left doctors out of his equation. He had produced numerous medical-journal articles, written by surgeons, advocating more time and the use of special techniques in amputation surgery, and bemoaning surgical errors, such as Tony had been victim to.

"There is already *push* within the medical community for upgrading amputation surgery," Bill had said; "upgrading prosthetics will create *pull* on this same issue—awareness will be roused, prosthetists and amputees both will be putting new pressures on doctors."

Bill had moved the leading prosthetist shaker forward, and then moved the physical therapist and doctor shakers along, as if being pulled.

"And the physical therapists get aligned in the process," he had concluded.

Jan continued to work Bill's words over in his mind. It was Jan's own argument, he knew, but infinitely clearer. Hearing it, like this, had given Jan the chance to play devil's advocate against himself. For nearly three hours he had tried to poke holes in Bill's theory. He couldn't.

Bill noted that Jan was nodding his head slowly, unconsciously—yes. Bill could not remember ever having worked so hard to convince someone that they were right.

"How come you won't let me eat dinner?" Bill said. "All you want to do is talk prosthetics. Stokosa, I'm hungry."

All through dinner Bill talked prosthetics, prosthetic legislation to be exact. He outlined his plan for implementing state licensing for prosthetists in Illinois—model legislation for other states to follow.

"But this is very long term," Bill said. "It takes years to pass legislation and more years for the effect to be felt. We have to do something now!"

"We?" Jan said.

"We," Bill said. "Look, I know you're a one-man show, up until now. But you've got a friend—and we need each other to do any good in this thing.

"And besides. . . ," Bill's voice had softened; he hesitated, then went ahead. "Jan, you've told me some things about your father. I've got to be grateful to Walter Stokosa, I *am* very grateful to him for training you so well, for teaching you to strive and to love excellence. But it doesn't sound as if he ever let anybody love him. It doesn't have to be that way. I'd have never made it without people caring for me. . .maybe you ought to let somebody care about you, it's no good to be so alone. Jan, you're so much alone. . ."

Jan was very quiet, uncomfortable. Nothing in his life had prepared him for such direct emotion. Yet Bill's words had rung true; they had felt almost good. He acknowledged what Bill had said with the slightest of nods. They sat quietly for a long moment.

And then Bill lifted them back to their previous mood. "Hey, Stokosa," he said, "my prosthetist says I have to lose some weight. Do you think anybody would tell him if I had a hot fudge sundae?"

After dessert, over coffee, Bill again became very serious. "What needs to happen," he said, "is something to help people right away. The licensing legislation is the right thing, long term, but it's too damned slow. Jan, I promised God if I ever got back on my feet I'd help others do the same. I want to do something *now*." Bill looked straight at Jan. "A nonprofit organization," he said, "to treat patients, to do research, to train prosthetists—I want prosthetists, of your caliber, on this earth before I die." Bill paused.

"Well," he said, "what shall we call it? The Stokosa Institute of Prosthetics?"

"Bill," Jan said, "what you're talking about would cost a *lot* of money."

"I've got a lot of money," Bill said.

"It could cost a million dollars, just to build."

"That's perfectly all right."

Jan stared across the table in disbelief. Bill met his eyes directly, and Jan knew that he was serious. And suddenly, so was Jan.

"My father should be here," Jan said. Tears brimmed in his eyes.

Bill nodded.

Jan took a deep breath. "All right, then," he said, "let's do it."

Bill offered his hand across the table. And Jan took it.

Author's Note

It is common that a considerable amount of time should elapse between the day an author finishes a book and the day it appears in the bookstore. The editing, layout, typesetting, cover art, etc., eat up more than a year, on the average. This is frustrating to the author. This book has been no exception.

But with Whole Again this predictable dark cloud contained the proverbial silver lining. It has afforded me the opportunity to update the story. Events since the time when the book originally ended have been dramatic, particularly in regard to proper amputation surgery: the final strand in the Gordian knot Bill Barr had sworn to cut through.

Epilogue

In March 1978 the IAP (Institute for the Advancement of Prosthetics) opened its doors. Located in Lansing, Michigan, it is the most modern, most fully equipped private prosthetics facility in the United States, perhaps in the world.

The institute was designed, from the slope of the surrounding terrain to the shape of the benches in the fabrication laboratory, by Jan Stokosa. There are many innovations, such as elevated parallel bars with adjacent videotape equipment.

The institute is bright and clean. A large aquarium covers one wall of the waiting room, hanging plants and framed pictures of Jan's patients fill the hallways. The examining rooms are large and private, with indirect lighting keeping glare from the patients' eyes.

In addition to the necessary space and equipment for providing prosthetic care, the institute has in-house physical therapy, a research laboratory, and a reference library.

The institute is staffed, besides office personnel, by three prosthetic technicians, recruited for the excellence of their work, from all over the United States.

Two fully subsidized interns are in residence, training to become prosthetists.

Jerry E. Villminot is the associate director. He has received the usual prosthetic training and certification, and also trained for a number of years with the late Walter Stokosa.

Jan Stokosa is the director.

The IAP is a nonprofit organization, governed by a board of directors. Bill Barr is the president of the board. Other members include Jerry Benson, Dr. Aaron Cahan, Norman Codo, the Honorable Benedict Garmisa, Dr. Howard Kurland, and Dr. Timothy Nugent.

In April 1978 Bill Barr held a press conference at the Bismark Hotel in Chicago. He announced the opening of the IAP, and he leveled criticism at the medical and prosthetic establishments. Several things ensued.

From Illinois alone, Bill received 374 calls, mostly from amputees in pain or suffering mobility problems. A number of these callers went on to seek help at the IAP.

The national prosthetics associations were bombarded with calls from the owners of prosthetic firms, complaining about the way they were being characterized. Moves were made within the associations to discredit the IAP and to remove the certification of Jan Stokosa.

At the same time, a number of individual prosthetists, also members of the associations, surfaced in support of Bill Barr's accusations and the goals of the IAP.

A public controversy was on.

Patients began to arrive at the institute. Edward Steiner of Chicago was one of the first. He had long experienced difficulty with his prosthesis and was one of those who called Bill after the press conference. He had viewed an account of Bill's remarks on a local television newscast.

After being fitted with a new prosthesis at the institute, Edward Steiner sent back an unsolicited letter, which read in part:

> I am so pleased with my new prosthesis that I feel

there aren't enough words in my vocabulary to express my feelings as to the work and concern for the betterment of the patient than has Jan Stokosa. He has made me realize there is more to an amputee's life than just sitting and feeling sorry for oneself. I now look forward to the walking, without pain, more now than before, hope to ride the bicycle again, which I wasn't able to do before, plan to go to sporting events, plays and shows. As far as I'm concerned, a new life has been opened to me which I truly thought was lost since my amputation.

More and more patients began to arrive at the institute, as word spread.

Charles Patterson, of Springfield, Ohio, was not an unusual case. A fireman, he had been badly burned and lost a part of his leg. For over a year prosthetists had told him his residual limb lacked enough skin to hold an artificial limb. He was in a wheelchair.

The institute fitted Charles Patterson with a prosthesis, and he returned to a normal life. As a matter of pride, he even passed the agility test required of prospective firemen. In an article in his hometown newspaper, he praised Jan and the institute. At the end of that article he said:

I want other people in my situation to see this and realize that there doesn't have to be a lot of pain—that they still can enjoy life. I once talked to an older man who was scared to death to stand up. If he stood up, the pain was almost unbearable. I'd like him to know that isn't how it has to be.

There were many patients and many stories. The *AMP* magazine featured an article about Jan and the IAP titled "Miracle at Lansing."

But certainly not every case was dramatic, nor did every patient have a history of failure. Some amputees who had already achieved good adjustments came to the institute to try to go even further. Zehavah Whitney—both legs missing, above the knee; already a winner of medals in amputee skiing—came to the institute. She was fitted with prostheses, especially designed for her athletic activities.

At a luncheon in Chicago, where she was named one of the city's five outstanding handicapped persons, she praised the work of the institute.

Despite the positive results with individual patients, the public controversy wore on. Some doctors, because of Bill Barr's criticism, recommended that amputees not go to the institute. Currents and countercurrents continued to run within the national prosthetic association.

The nonprofit status of the IAP was challenged and delayed, making the procurement of contributions and government grants next to impossible—and the IAP's operation was proving expensive. Zehavah Whitney's prostheses, for instance, cost the institute over $12,000 to produce. The funding agency which pays for Zehavah's prostheses allowed $3,000, leaving $9,000 for the institute to absorb. The situation was similar in many cases.

Bill Barr continued single-handedly to subsidize the work of the IAP, and he continued to speak out.

On September 24 the story of amputee Jerry Benson, the "super vet," came to great public attention. His story was soon to merge with those of Bill Barr and Jan Stokosa.

In 1969 nineteen-year-old Jerry Benson was on patrol, as a marine, in Vietnam. A 122-mm. rocket exploded nearby. His left leg was badly torn by the shrapnel. Still conscious, he watched medics, with razor blades and alcohol, amputate his leg below the knee.

224

Back in the States he was fitted with a prosthesis at a veterans hospital and given a long list of things he would never be able to do. "Watch me," he said.

For the next nine years he sought help, visiting doctors and prosthetists. But mostly he ended up helping himself. He read medical journals and prescribed his own revision surgery—a procedure called "Ertl," joining the bones in his stump together to make a single, broader contact point. It helped. He had a dozen prostheses built, in five different states. Finally he began to design his own limbs and, one way and another, had them built. There was improvement. He could do many of the things he had been told he would never do. Still, he felt he had only begun.

In 1978 he met eight-year-old Cheryl Arlowe. She had lost both her feet in an accident when she was three. She wanted, more than anything, to run. The prosthetic devices she wore barely allowed her to walk.

Jerry told her if she believed strongly enough, she would run. And he would help her.

A short time later, on September 24, Jerry Benson entered the Mayor Daley Marathon in Chicago. He wore a bright yellow T-shirt with SUPER VET emblazoned across the front. His plan was to draw public attention to Cheryl's problem, and to his problem—and to the problems of all amputees. He told the press, before the race, "If we have the money and the technology to let a man walk on the moon, then surely we have the money and technology to let a little eight-year-old girl run on this earth if she has the will to do so. And if we don't understand which represents the greater achievement of mankind, may God forgive us all."

Nine miles into the marathon Jerry's stump was bruised and bleeding, and his self-designed prosthesis ceased to

225

function properly. He completed the last seventeen miles of the race on crutches. In all, 26.2 miles in 9 hours and 47 minutes.

Bill Jauss of the *Chicago Tribune* wrote a feature about Jerry. The wire services picked up the story and it went nationwide.

Jerry received a total of one call, offering help: from Jan Stokosa at the IAP.

By mid-December both Cheryl and Jerry were wearing new prostheses made at the IAP. Bill Jauss did a follow-up on Cheryl and Jerry for the *Chicago Tribune*. It appeared on Sunday, December 17. It was on the front page, with a large picture of Cheryl and Jerry. It began like this:

THE REAL JOY OF RUNNING
By Bill Jauss

Jerry Benson's voice, coming over the phone, choked with joy. His five words told of the greatest Christmas gift he could possibly have received.

"Guess what? Cheryl can run!"

That was several days ago. Thursday, on the Eisenhower grammar school playground behind Benson's South Holland home, eight-year-old Cheryl Arlowe ran a footrace against Benson over an icy strip of cement.

Cheryl ran on two artificial plastic legs. They were designed, handcrafted, and fitted by a Lansing, Mich., genius named Jan J. Stokosa.

"I beat you, Jerry," cried the second-grader from Nativity School. "Now you have to buy me a hot dog."

Tears welled up in Benson's dark eyes.

"Cheryl," he said, "is probably the only human being in the world today who can do that."...

Again the wire services picked up the story. Soon Jerry was being invited to appear on television and radio talk shows. He accepted the invitations and spoke out about prosthetics, and about Jan and the IAP. Jerry was now running twenty miles, without significant pain.

A resolution praising Jerry's courage and reiterating Jerry's praise of Jan and the IAP was read into the *Congressional Record.*

The controversy sparked by Bill Barr and Jan Stokosa was beginning to heat up. And Jerry Benson was the point man.

In less than a year the prosthetics industry itself began seriously to listen.

On January 22, 1979, at the Conoven Hotel in Miami, Florida, Jan Stokosa, Bill Barr, Tony Barr, Hon. Benedict Garmisa, and Jerry Benson met with representatives of the American Orthotic and Prosthetic Association and its two divisions: the American Academy of Orthotists and Prosthetists, and the American Board of Certification.

From this and subsequent meetings came an association resolution regarding the improvement and upgrading of prosthetic care. The resolution was passed. It read:

> I move that the American Academy of Orthotists and Prosthetists go on record by a vote of the majority of members present at this meeting that we are:
>
> (1) In favor of proper enforcement of existing handicapped laws regarding requirements for physical facilities; these laws have been enacted by federal, state, county, and local government agencies.
>
> (2) In favor of action by states to enact meaningful licensure laws for prosthetists and orthotists, and will work to develop a model licensure act. Generally

speaking, the enactment of such a licensure law in a state would create a commission that would consist of representatives of the affected interests, i.e., orthotists, prosthetists, therapists, physicians, consumers, and public interest members. Such a commission should also seek professional assistance from a professional examination service.

(3) In favor of all efforts made to educate private and government reimbursers as to what constitutes a high level of prosthetic and orthotic service and the reimbursement requirements to provide such high level service.

The year 1979 continued to be one of impact and achievement. The IAP completed its first twelve months of operation, having treated three hundred patients from over half of the fifty United States, as well as patients from Canada, Mexico, and England. Inquiries were received from as far away as Israel and the Soviet Union.

The IAP was granted nonprofit status by the Internal Revenue Service.

Super vet Jerry Benson again entered the Chicago Mayor Daley Marathon. He ran the full 26.2 miles on an IAP prosthesis, reporting no pain.

Zehavah Whitney set out on an international skiing tour, demonstrating her IAP prostheses and her skiing ability to other amputees.

The Honorable Benedict Garmisa drafted model prosthetic legislation that was introduced in the Illinois legislature.

And Bill Barr underwent the revision surgery that Jan Stokosa had suggested at their very first meeting, the final step in Bill's ten-year odyssey.

During 1978 and early 1979 Bill and Jan undertook a

concerted effort to find a surgeon willing to do and capable of doing reconstruction surgery on Bill's stump. Jan's prosthetic solution had given Bill mobility and a large measure of relief from pain. But some pain remained.

It is ironic that of the many amputees helped by Jan and the burgeoning IAP, all made possible by Bill Barr's efforts, it was Bill himself who had found less than a final solution.

The problems in securing proper surgery were formidable. The type of surgery Jan envisioned was not to his knowledge being performed anywhere in the United States. The reconstruction techniques he believed Bill required had been pioneered in Germany around 1918 by a surgeon named John Ertl (the same Ertl after whom the surgical procedure Jerry Benson read of and prescribed for himself had been named). The techniques of John Ertl, although dramatically successful, had fallen into disuse.

The Ertl above-knee surgery was far more complex than the Ertl below-knee surgery Jerry Benson had undergone, which complicated the problem Jan and Bill faced: even knowing what operation they desired, finding the surgeon to perform it was next to impossible.

Bill Barr, just emerging from a ten-year nightmare in which doctors had played no small part, was not about to go ahead with the surgery until he found the *right* man.

During 1978 and early 1979 several promising leads were followed up, including attempts to locate a European surgeon. Nothing materialized.

Then in October the IAP received a new patient from Illinois, a routine occurrence. But the prescription the patient carried was not routine at all. The name at the bottom caused Jan's heart to beat rapidly. He stared in disbelief. Could someone be playing a very poor joke?

The name John Ertl was signed to the prescription!

Jan sat down. Even if John Ertl had done his pioneering work while in his twenties, he would now be over one hundred years old. Then it came to Jan, of all people, slowly: a son!

It turned out to be two sons, John and William, both surgeons. Both had trained at their father's side in Germany. They had immigrated, along with John Ertl, Sr., to the United States in 1951. John Ertl, Sr. died only six weeks later.

The Ertl brothers had their practice in Hinsdale, Illinois, less than an hour's drive from Bill Barr's home. And, yes, of course, they could perform the Ertl above-knee reconstruction procedures.

Bill visited the Ertls immediately. He found two doctors; both were warm and empathetic men. There was an immediate rapport between Bill and the Ertls. Before he left, Bill heard a father-and-sons story—although vastly different—to rival that of the Stokosas.

On November 12, 1979, Bill entered the Hinsdale Suburban Hospital in Illinois. Dojna and Tony and Robin were with him. Even with the Ertls handling the surgery, Bill found himself frightened and doubting. He had been here before, he felt, so many times.

On November 15 the surgery was performed by both John and William Ertl. Jan Stokosa was present in the operating theater. For complicated medical reasons, Bill was unable to receive a general anesthetic. A spinal injection was given and he remained conscious during the operation, truly a final test of his nerve.

The operation itself consisted of four main components: (1) excess nerves were removed from the stump, (2) arteries and veins were separated, (3) the periosteum (a thin bone-covering skin) was stretched down to cover the fe-

230

mur in Bill's thigh; tiny islands of bone from the upper femur were then transplanted into the periosteum, these to create a protective bone flap on this bearing point, and (4) the muscles in Bill's thigh were repositioned and stretched down and joined, forming a cushion, over the end of the femur.

The operation in everyone's judgment, most importantly Bill's, was a success. Within days the pain in Bill's stump was diminished.

Jan referred seven patients, with long-standing problems such as Bill's, to the Ertls in the following month. Prior to meeting Jan and Bill, amputations had made up less than ten percent of the Ertls' practice. Already this figure has increased.

Bill Barr is doing well, very well. Nick Murphy, the friend who first came to Bill's aid as he lay on the pavement after the bombing, said it all recently: Bill is even more dynamic and committed to life than he was before the bombing; it's a miracle.

A final note. A bronze bust of Walter Stokosa has been placed in the reception area at the IAP. The inscription reads:

> Walter J. Stokosa, in his lifetime, exhibited an unsurpassed dedication to the field of prosthetics. He was dedicated to excellence in all aspects of the field, and participated fully in each. He was both practitioner and researcher. In 1971, he died due to the effect of smoke inhalation suffered when a molding oven in his research lab malfunctioned.
>
> The Institute for the Advancement of Prosthetics, Inc., is dedicated to his memory.

So much has been accomplished in such a short time: promising initiatives brought about by a handful of men. But the real battle to translate these initiatives into real and widespread improvements in the lives of handicapped persons has only begun.